The Spirits Speak on Success

Sixty Must Read, Candid Commentaries on Success as Told Through the Eyes and the Essence of the Spirit Realm.

Shared with and scribed by

Diane Marie Ford

Book Cover designed by Rachel Dunham, Your Brand Therapy
Diane Marie Ford's Cover Photograph by Danielle Mulcahy, DanielleMulcahy.com
Cover photographs of Frank Sinatra, Janis Joplin, Lucille Ball and Abraham Lincoln courtesy of Wikimedia.

Cover photographs of Leah Ford © 1989, 2017 Diane Marie Ford, and Buddynwolf, the corgi © 2004, 2017 Diane Marie Ford.

Planet of Plentitude Publishing/The Spirits Speak Series
First Edition Volume 1 ~ Printed in the United States of America

ISBN-10: 0998972800
ISBN-13: 9780998972800

Library of Congress Control Number: 2014917908
Planet of Plentitude Publishing
Middleborough, MA

Dedication

She brought me into this world and led by example. Strong, loving, fearless and tender, there wasn't anything she couldn't accomplish once she put her mind to it. Passion and purpose fueled her; a sense of accomplishment drove her. She continues to provide inspiration and guidance and a good kick in the butt when needed. My number one, go-to guide and confidante in the afterlife, my mother, Leah Ford, née Bibeau, I dedicate this book to you. (She is seated front and center on the cover.)

Contents

Foreword

"Diane Marie Ford's *The Spirits Speak on Success* never stops giving. This sensory rich deeply moving collaboration with spirits is astonishing, down-to-earth, and uniquely insightful. If you have ever wondered about the meaning of success, you'll not find a more diverse and thought-provoking gathering of ideas and perspectives from the 'afterlife', the experts on the topic from beginning to end, literally.

Each 'speaker' leaves no holds barred in their frank opinions and compassionate yet firm advice to those of us still here in form. We can change for the better... Not only do these spirits want to help us, but they are readily available to teach and guide us if we simply open up to listen. Ms. Ford provides both the platform and the podium. This landmark work stands out as an unforgettable page-turner and living guide."

Katharine Gilpin
Creative Healing Artist, SoundBody Therapist

Acknowledgments

The Spirits Speak on Success says it all. Thank you, my dear contributing spirits... my 'spirit connections' – your willingness to show up and share the intimate details of your perspectives about success made this, our first book in The Spirits Speak series, possible. May our symbiotic collaborations continue to serve as a platform for self-expression, awareness, education and love.

The wind beneath my wings, head cheerleader, steadfast editor, and partner through the ages, Katharine... I need not say more. You revel in my success as I revel in yours, and *yes!* – We have made it to print!

Marinna Rose, your belief in me and *all things possible* guided me to the end result, which you 'saw' early on. Your insight and love are ever appreciated.

Rachel Dunham, designer extraordinaire and friend, you continue to blow me away! Your knack of transforming that, which I cannot see nor speak, into magnificent expressions of my deepest thoughts, never ceases to amaze me. You exquisitely capture the essence and message of this book with your brilliantly designed cover. Wowza.

My friends and family, those unnamed yet in my heart (you know who you are) and those who have heard about me writing this book for the past four years and have been awaiting its arrival, I thank you for your encouragement, support, and belief in me and this project. 'This' was a long time coming, and it would never have arrived had I not been supported and held by each and every one of you. I am so grateful.

Introduction

Do you find yourself struggling to reach a level of success without knowing your definition of success?

Would you like to have a clearer understanding of the meaning of success?

Are you so wrapped up in the pursuit of material gains/goods that you have lost sight of the *little things* in life?

Have you attained colossal success and now sit on top of the world in misery and with regrets?

Has the attainment of success been completely blown out of proportion?

Do you sometimes wonder since "you can't take it with you," what is the pursuit of success all about?

What if you had the resources available at your fingertips to ask these and many other questions about success of those who now dwell in the spirit realm and who have lived through and experienced these scenarios... would you explore the possibilities, connect and seek their expertise?

Imagine being able to learn from others' past triumphs or failures, joys, or sorrows. Then imagine how those teachings could serve to better counsel you now in the present. Our ancestors and loved ones in spirit are uniquely positioned to shed a different kind of light on our earthly struggles and pursuits of success. They offer a one-of-a-kind reflection on the nature of success.

In my capacity as a certified holistic counselor, I guide my clients through various life struggles and obstacles. Though I have counseled on many issues, from addictions to low self-worth and everything in between, there is one topic, or issue, that either always comes up or never comes up yet shows up everywhere: the concept of success.

While reflecting on the meaning and interpretations of success and winding down the sixtieth year of my life, an idea popped into my ever-inquisitive mind: what if I were to call upon my favorite, number one, go-to guide in spirit, my mother, Leah, to assist me with a project? After all, her help in navigating through the afterlife is priceless.

What if I were to consciously connect for the remaining sixty days of my sixtieth year with sixty spirits and invite them to share their definitions of success. There are, after all, sixty seconds in a minute, sixty minutes in an hour, and this would be the final sixty days of my sixtieth year. There was something fascinating about the prospect. The number sixty beckoned me to explore this route. I was compelled to begin this project. I was also compelled to explore the connection with the number sixty.

Turning to Doreen Virtue's *Angel Numbers 101* book, which "clearly explains how to receive accurate messages from your angels and heavenly loved ones," I read the meaning of the number sixty and received my message loud and clear: "You are vacillating between focusing upon Spirit and the material world. This number is a call for you to balance your focus, and always remember that Spirit is your source and the force behind everything in your life." The countdown commenced and we (my mother, the spirits, and I) were off and running!

Here is what it looked like: each and every day I retreated to my sacred office space and lit a candle. In deep reflection and quiet meditation, I allowed my energy to flow, unencumbered by preconceived notions or thoughts. As I drifted deeper, my energy soared higher, and with pen in hand, I began to write what I 'heard'. I wrote and wrote, very quickly, unaware of what I was writing – knowing only that I must continue to do so until the energy was complete and the connection terminated. (Some may refer to this as channeling or automatic writing. Me? I refer to it as transcribing messages.)

Amazed by the visitors and their messages, I read each entry aloud (to another human being). Then – and only then – did I feel the impact and import of what had taken place. This was beyond my wildest imaginings. This was a service I was providing for those in the spirit realm, the afterlife. They shared their deepest, darkest secrets and greatest lessons learned. They vented, expressed, and graciously provided their best kept stories and advice on how to approach and handle success and the pursuit thereof.

Each and every day for sixty consecutive days, I was excited to begin the process and surprised to host a plethora of spirits, from celebrities to family members and friends. I was amazed by their visits and individual interpretations of success. They trusted me enough to hold the space for them to bare their souls, and that, in and of itself, was an honor and a privilege. While many shared light and lively contributions to the meaning of success, others, whose stories were not so upbeat, had valuable lessons to impart as well. The shared common denominators were faith, hope, belief and love.

May this book serve as your own personal guide to help you gain a deeper understanding of the age-old question "is there more to life than meets the eye?" and assist you in living a deeper, richer, and more successful life now, in the present. Help yourself to the wisdom and insight of those who have gone before us and now pave the way and hold the light. They share their life lessons to teach us how it is possible to change one's mind-set and beliefs...one step at a time. From Janis Joplin, who insists there is no "other side", to my dog, Buddy, who summarizes his interpretation of success as "a good belly rub" – this book provides something for everyone.

PAUSE FOR REFLECTION & PURPOSE

Before embarking upon this journey, please pause and give thought to your definition of success. Grant yourself the space and time to compose and write down your responses...

Do you consider yourself a success in your own eyes? If so, describe what that looks like and what feelings are associated with being successful. If not, what will it take for you to achieve success (e.g., meaningful relationships, deeper love of self, more money, etc.)?

_____

_____

_____

_____

_____

_____

_____

_____

_____

_____

_____

How easily do you allow another's definition or perception of success to define you, influence your actions, and impact your lifestyle? How does that feel? (e.g., authentic, overwhelming, expansive, joyful, contracting, or satisfying?)

_____

_____

_____

_____

_____

_____

_____

_____

_____

_____

_____

_____

_____

_____

_____

_____

_____

_____

_____

_____

_____

_____

_____

What are the little things in life you may have a tendency to overlook in your efforts to strive for success?

_____

_____

_____

_____

_____

_____

_____

_____

_____

_____

_____

_____

_____

_____

_____

_____

_____

_____

_____

_____

_____

_____

_____

_____

If you have yet to achieve the level of success you know is possible, what will it take to do so, and how will you know when you have achieved that desired level? In what ways will your life change, what will you feel and look like, and how will those around you be impacted?

_____

_____

_____

_____

_____

_____

_____

_____

_____

_____

_____

_____

_____

_____

_____

_____

_____

_____

_____

_____

_____

The Spirits Speak on Success...Countdown

Day 60

Myth busting –

You only get one life.

We are all going crazy trying to create perfection in this lifetime.

Progress, not perfection.

All lifetimes are cumulative.

Exponential.

Sum of the parts.

Layered.

Do your best, but/and enjoy the ride – the show – take time to smell the roses.

The beauty is in the details.

[Taborri Spirit Child]

[Taborri Spirit Child is a young soul who is near and dear to my heart. She has been showing up in my life a great deal as of late. Insightful, quick to the point, and spot on with her messages. She is a delightful energy who tells it like it is.]

Day 59

Define your own success.

Only you can define your own success.

Take the pressure off. There is so much pressure to *be*, *do*, *have*, in the physical world these days – unlike anything I had ever experienced. Sure, we had our share of challenges – the Great Depression, food lines, making due, hand-me-downs – but the pressure in the twenty-first century is like a pressure cooker.

It's no wonder people are causing mass damage, and mother earth is revolting. Too much pressure.

Don't allow others to define your success.

One woman's success is another woman's mess.

This is your life and your choices.

Be clear as to what success looks, tastes, and feels like.

While I was quite content as a stay-at-home mother, caring for many children – mostly infants – there was a gnawing in my stomach. I made due. I defined my own success and learned how to take on tasks that challenged me – building chicken coops, small sheds, designing and planting gardens. I was a success in my own right. I created my own happiness surrounded by the people I loved and the things I loved to do.

What does success look like for you?

Take the time to become very clear about your vision – your goal – and then create the outcome you wish or desire to have.

In hindsight – we are far more powerful and capable than we allow ourselves to be. It's so easy to think *less than* and belittle ourselves. We possess the vision, the insight, yet tapping into it – igniting it, setting it to flame is another story in and of itself.

I didn't realize the totality of everything I could have been, because I did not have the vision in the physical form.

Maybe it's something you acquire only when you are in spirit form? I'm not sure, but I'm here to share that now.

I sure hope this helps.

Enjoy!

[Leah 'Ma' Ford]

['Ma' Ford is my number one go-to guide and greatest inspiration. She taught me well while she walked the earth plane and continues to teach me – especially about making due. Through the years I have learned that while making due for those of her generation was a step above her parents' generation, my generation deserves to raise the bar and live more abundantly. Thank you, Ma, for teaching me how to do just that.]

- Generations for individuals born in the United States of America:

  Hard Timers 1890–1908 (Grandparents')
  Good Warriors 1909–1928 (Parents')
  Lucky Few 1929–1945

(Also referred to as Traditionalists or Silent Generation: Born 1945 and before.)
Baby Boomers 1946–1964 (Mine)
Generation X 1965–1976
Millennials or Gen Y 1977– 1995
Gen Z or Centennials 1996– and later.*

*Information obtained from various resources.

Day 58

Speak up for success. Don't let anyone take away your voice – rob you of your message, purpose, identity, soul.

Don't get lost in your shadow self.

To repurpose, which is a new way of re-languaging my message…

Shine your life. Live your purpose. Dance in your divinity.

I stepped aside and allowed others to strip me of my success. My outer demeanor and appearance was that of a cold-hearted, up-tight, ~~unhappy~~, strict woman. I asked you to strike the word unhappy because I never gave anyone the appearance of being unhappy, even though deep inside I was miserable.

I thought – no – I pretended – <u>success</u> was determined by <u>things</u>.

Nice things.

The number of nice things one accumulated in their life time – the more, the greater in number, or by appearance sake one had – the more successful they were.

I allowed others to take my voice away, strip me of my dreams. So I created what I thought were my dreams. They were not.

I was miserable. My furniture was covered in plastic.

I, too, was covered in plastic.

Unable to reveal my true self.

A plastic face.

I adapted to wearing mine well.

On the outside, my life and world appeared to be perfect.

Immaculate.

Ideal.

Happy.

Inside I was crying. I was devoid of all real feelings – I never allowed myself to get in touch with them. I couldn't. To do so would have caused me to fail – and to reveal my true self, dreams, hopes, and aspirations would have appeared to have been selfish. I never could have allowed that.

I went so far within, that my family had to shock treat me to return me to my senses.

I never did.

I never returned.

I burrowed within my sorrow and, on some level, found peace and happiness and comfort there.

Success requires a strong voice.

Success requires backbone and courage.

It is possible to reach the pinnacle of your success.

Success also requires clarity – be clear with your definition of success and what it means to you.

And never, never ever allow anyone to rob you of your success.

Success requires strength. We all possess that strength.

What are YOU willing to do to nurture and build that strength?

Speak out – Speak up!

[Anonymous]

[This feminine energy, replete with glorious messages of hope and expression, chooses to remain anonymous to protect her family and keep her secrets safe. I am happy she has found the courage to speak her piece, hopefully helping others to do the same. Perhaps one day she will completely shed her fear and come forth in all her glory.]

Day 57

Success should not be confused with popularity.

Oftentimes, in order to become successful you jeopardize your popularity. You give up fame, fortune, status in one area to achieve success in another.

Not by popular vote.

By conviction.

Conviction must play an important role in your quest for success. I don't mean financial success, or success which will render you popular among your peers. I am referring to success of your soul.

Doing the right things not necessarily at the right time or due to popular vote or because it is what the people may or may not want or approve of in the moment, but because you are steadfast – remaining steadfast to your own convictions.

Your personal beliefs should steer you along the path or road of success and those beliefs serve as your master – your starboard beacon and fortitude.

Do not be led astray or drift away from your soul's purpose, which is led by your beliefs and the other way around. Your beliefs and your soul's purpose are one – and they are very closely intertwined.

Do not allow public opinion to sway you nor taint or color that which your soul knows to be your truth. It is your truth, and your truth will set you free. Honestly. And acting on your truth will bring success. Not popularity in all cases – but success. You will know when you are successful or have reached the level or place of success, because it will be in your soul – it will click. It will cause a deep stirring. That is success.

No one knows what the future may hold – we never know. We act on faith and belief, and if our soul is allowed to rule, we will never, ever be led astray. Even in death.

[Abraham Lincoln]

[Though I questioned him at first – wondering why he (Abraham Lincoln) would come through to me – he, in turn, asked me why I would question and not simply believe. I am asking others to put aside their cynicism for the sake of consciously connecting. Shouldn't I be acting in the same manner and with the same faith? President Lincoln made it clear that by questioning his contribution, I was questioning not only myself but the process – and he strongly suggested I step aside and out of my own way. And so I did.]

Day 56

Success comes in many different sizes, shapes, and colors. To me, a dog, (but you know that) success is a funny thing.

When you humans, two-leggeds, speak of success, my eyes twinkle and my heart skips a beat. I believe we view it differently.

Success is a warm bed. A belly full of kibble. Someone to love you and someone you can love.

Success is companionship – being part of a pack, a family.

Success means being able to do what you want to when you want to.

Carefree.

Worry-free.

Heavenly.

Success – true success – in my estimation and from what I've seen, is comfort, joy, love.

It's not about what you have or own – or how much of what you have or own – it's more about how you feel and what you feel.

Sort of like peace.

Success is like peace.

Peaceful and complete.

Requiring nothing else.

Whole, perfect. Complete, care-free.

A warm bed.

A companion.

A full belly.

A good belly rub.

A state of quiet meditation.

Being lost in a dream.

Feeling safe, secure, loved.

A sense of belonging.

A good walk in a park or a run with other dogs.

A belly rub – did I mention a belly rub?

Success is a good belly rub.

Quiet, complete, loved.

Success is being part of a family who loves you.

Success is love.

If you have love and you are loved and you can love – you are successful.

[Buddynwolf, a.k.a. Buddy, our beloved dog.]

[*Sir Buddynwolf Rowan Crowfeather GilpinFord, a.k.a. Buddy, was a magical canine companion and buddy beyond words. His corgi essence fills my soul and brings a smile to my heart. I delight in connecting with our animal companions and not only cherish but value their insight. Wise beyond comprehension, Buddy is a great mentor and confidante. I am elated he came through and shared.*]

(A photograph of Buddy, in one of his favorite positions, is on the back cover.)

Day 55

Success is the color pink.

Pink represents positive thinking.

Positive feeling.

I have always surrounded myself in the color pink. Pink and positive affirmations.

But you know that.

I was the first woman general manager in the 'herstory' (history) of insurance. Was I successful? No. I was a trailblazer, and being a trailblazer is far more of an achievement than being successful.

Success breeds success.

So what does that mean?

I have always believed in being true to yourself – your roots – and never, ever forgetting where you came from. But you know that, too.

Success, to me, is defined as integrity.

What does a woman have to do to be deemed successful?

She has to be true to herself first and her beliefs first and foremost.

She has to be in full integrity – thoughts, words, actions, deeds.

A truly successful woman mentors well. She helps others become their very best.

A truly successful woman has a knack of identifying potential in another and helping to hone that person's potential. A protégé.

Let's move on.

True success is more of a feeling than a tangible item.

It is reflected in the way you walk – the way you treat others – firm yet soft, loving yet tough.

The long stick. Remember the ruler I used to threaten to hit you over the head with? [*Laughs*] Caring enough about a person to mentor her or him, that is the feeling of success.

I saw your potential – I brought that out through firm, yet loving actions and mentoring.

I mentored many.

I loved mentoring others.

Like a mother bird taking her young under her wings and doing everything a mother bird does – until her fledgling is pushed out of the nest.

Would anyone refer to the mother bird as cruel or abusive? I think not.

Success is a state of mind, and it is a reward for the feeling you carry deep inside.

A feeling of accomplishing something bigger than yourself through a power greater than yourself.

The power always belongs to God. But you know that, too.

Success is a gift you give to yourself. Success is made to be shared and feel humbled about.

No one (woman or man) gains/finds/reaches/achieves success by themselves.

Success is not a solo project.

Success is a team endeavor. It takes many to achieve success.

Success is always to be shared. There's no sense in success if you do not share it.

Joy is success, and sharing success is joyful.

The purpose of achieving success – no matter how you choose to define it – is to celebrate and share.

It is for the greater good. Everything I achieved, goals achieved, successes won or earned, was for the greater good.

You may not have understood that then, though I imagine within the haze you *did* know that on some level.

A successful person should never be idealized, adored, nor looked up to.

A successful person should remain humble, remember her roots and all those who have gone before her, and she should always be grateful for her many blessings, making sure to share along the way.

Success breeds success.

I do believe in reciprocity, and I do believe we can share the good, the wealth, and the wisdom – always and from whatever plane of existence we dwell.

[Jean Gorman]

[My first mentor, Jean Gorman, left an indelible impression upon my heart and instilled a sense of direction in my life. This woman walked her talk and talked her walk. Though she mentioned she was not a success, I do believe her humility led her to respond as such. She was a trailblazer and a fine teacher. She helped me to move forward and taught me to "never forget where I came from". Jean lived and breathed "success breeds success". I was compelled to research that quote and found that – success breeds success – because "If you teach someone how to be successful

they will become successful and they will teach others to become successful." Yes, Jean, you taught me well, and for this, among other lessons, I remain most grateful and thankful.]

Day 54

I don't know much about success, but I do know how you can be successful and that is to have a completely pure heart and soul and a one-on-one relationship with your god, as you define him or even her – although I believe my God is a He.

My life was dedicated to my children – raising them, loving them, and teaching them right from wrong.

Dedicated to my family. Loving them, caring for them, and being the best mother I could possibly be. It also included my life – that is, or the existence or goals of my life, to be a good, attentive daughter and steadfast friend to my sisters.

My husband's life was cut short. I lived in darkness and despair for quite some time. The love of my family, especially my sister, whose name I chose to not reveal, sustained me and carried me through the pain and agony of my tragic loss.

I consider myself a success because I endured that loss and carried on.

I found deeper meaning to life and developed a deeper connection *to* and love *for* my God.

I got to know God on a level unlike that which my Catholic upbringing taught. A rich, deep, loving relationship. I considered that as wealth – a newfound wealth – at a time when my soul was bankrupt.

I built upon that wealth and made daily deposits into my spiritual bank account, and as I did, my spiritual wealth increased.

I came to have, possess, own, an unshakable faith and spiritual wealth beyond measure.

There is no way I could possibly put into words the feeling of my newfound spiritual wealth, which, in hindsight, might very well be deemed as a success of sorts.

I suppose.

I just know the beauty of it all transformed me – uplifted me to levels I never dreamt of being possible and filled my heart and head with joy, love, and unlimited possibilities.

I left this earth plane in the still of the night – like a thief moving into a new dimension. Surrounded by my herd of cats – who were bewildered and felt betrayed – they knew not what had happened to me. (We are blessed and reside together again. This time everything is much different. Unlimited resources.)

I suppose on some level I cashed in my wealth – bought a ticket to my father's land. A time and place without judgment or fear.

I took my spiritual wealth and purchased a one-way ticket. I imagine, again, in retrospect, had I not made daily deposits in my spiritual account, I would not have had the currency to cash in – in exchange for my ticket.

So in a sense, it was me who decided to take leave of this planet as we know it.

Caution: be careful what you wish for.

Craft your success plan carefully.

We are mightier than the sword, and we do manifest our desires.

I am happy. I am with my heavenly family. I am successful to that end.

[Anonymous]

[My aunt, who wishes to remain anonymous, walked softly and carried a big message. She was quiet, knowing, unassuming. Her mission later in life was to deliverer and share God's word. She was spiritually wealthy beyond measure and shared the bounty of her wealth with all. It is comforting to know she continues to shower us with her wealth.]

Day 53

Success is showing up.

It is having the courage to get out on the stage of life and simply be.

We all possess the beauty and wisdom, which makes us magnificent beings, but, yet, we oftentimes give into fear, which diminishes our light and keeps us playing small.

When you were just a child – three years of age – you refused to participate in your dance recital. Although we had rehearsed for weeks, and you knew your routine (and I lovingly labored over the sewing machine, making all the costumes, pink in color and oh so cute) when it came time for you to step out onto the stage – you refused. You flat-out absolutely refused. You could be a little devil at times, you know?

We needed to go on with the show – so I allowed you to get the better of me and in doing so – I unknowingly allowed fear to rule your life at such a young age. And in hindsight – that, my dear, was a grave mistake. I regret having put beliefs into motion on that day.

I chose not to allow that to happen again. (And you know exactly what I mean and what I am referring to even if you can't pinpoint it exactly – I know you understand the essence of my message.)

So you want to talk about success?

Success in hindsight? Or success from my current vantage point? Or better yet, how success may serve you now – at this point in time?

Being successful does not involve being fearful.

Success knows no boundaries – nor limitations.

Success does not give in to "but I can't", "what if" "_____" (I fail, I'm lousy, they laugh, etc..? – fill in the blank.)

Success is you at your finest hour.

Success is saying *yes* without second-guessing yourself.

Success is believing in yourself no matter what.

Success is taking a chance.

Success is going out on a limb.

Success is living life without terms, conditions, fears.

Success is believing.

Success is loving.

Success is simply being yourself.

So, daughter Diane, simply be yourself, and consider yourself a success.

[Leah 'Ma' Ford]

[When the idea of _____ (fill in the blank) is planted deep into consciousness at an early age, it leads to a belief that we _____ (fill in the blank).

My mother made a decision to spare me from whatever fear I was experiencing at the tender and impressionable age of three. This was a decision deeply rooted and grounded in love. While she made the best decision in that moment for me, her terrified child unable to step onto the stage, neither one of us knew that decision would set up a belief that would influence me as time marched on. It is said hindsight is twenty-twenty.

I am grateful my mother is watching my back, and we continue to learn together. Thanks, Ma!]

Day 52

Success is staying sober.

Addictions appear to be a commonplace among us when we are human.

Everyone has some sort of addiction.

Food, drugs, truth, no truth, addicted to low self-esteem, or anything which sub-consciously holds us back from living our true potential – our best life.

It may be fear of our own greatness or fear of being our best self. Because, after all, if we become our best self – what is left?

What would we strive for if we achieved our true potential?

What would life be like if it were everything? If we reached the pinnacle of our success – then what would we do? What would we strive for?

So, we create ways to hold ourselves back.

For some, that might be with an addiction.

We create ideas in our minds that life isn't everything it's cracked up to be. We lament our lousy life and turn to something to make us (or so we think) feel better. Better than what? Better than Ezra?

We make ourselves believe that we have a chemical deficiency – because to believe it is a choice – that we choose to be addicted – would cause the whole house of cards to collapse right in front of us, but, more importantly – in front of others.

So, we convince ourselves that these choices we have made are out of our control, and maybe, just maybe, a drug will help – a prescribed drug, that is – because then it's legal (wink, wink) and off we go.

We're running and operating on high octane fuel, and our lives are never the same.

When we later realize the drugs aren't helping, we decide to return to the old self-help stuff – alcohol, illegal drug – and wham! Before we know it we're suffering from a depression so deep and heavy there's no escaping. You can't even move – let alone escape.

So, within this deep, dark, dank, heavy dimension you wander.

If I had allowed myself to be brilliant – to go for it and say *to hell* with what happens when I become all I am destined to become – when you throw caution to the wind and say fuck the naysayers (the loudest naysayer being yourself, of course) and pursue your true calling – which oftentimes does not follow on the path of least resistance – do you shine in light, feel light as a feather, and soar like a feather on the back of a bird?

I would think yes, but that thought always terrified me – I laid low – just got by – allowed "just enough" of my brilliance to shine through, and fought like hell to succumb to my greatness. Too, too scary.

In retrospect, I wished I had had the 'balls' to be brilliant.

I believe true success is becoming 'ballsy' enough to be brilliant, and rather than being afraid of that process and the end result – which of course is your own, pure, unadulterated brilliance – you have the guts and determination to shine and be your best.

For some of us that's really scary or unimaginable.

So maybe part of being successful is helping others to realize their beautiful selves and helping them step into success as well.

Success means staying sober.

I didn't need all these drugs – I set myself up to believe I did. I didn't.

['The Walrus']

[My old friend and confidante challenged me by adding, "Go ahead, Ford – publish that!" So, my dear Walrus, consider it done.]

Day 51

♫ Sing, sing a song, make it simple to last your whole life long, don't worry it may not be good enough for everyone else to sing – so sing, sing a song. ♪ *

Funny – odd – I sang those lyrics yet never believed in them. No, maybe I did believe in them, and that's why I sang them – I wanted them to be true, I struggled with believing they could be [true].

I piggyback on the previous written sentiments (no names to protect anonymity), and when referring to me you may simply say I was part of a brother sister duet, popular in the seventies – because I really want to spare my brother's sorrow or remembrance.

Sure we were hot.

We were on fire.

Burt B. was amazed with/by my liquid gold voice and ease of delivering a tune.

The drumming part was the frosting on the cake (and I know you secretly harbor desires of being a drummer and, by the way, you have the beat); however, moving right along, I also know you have been a fan of mine for decades and decades and processed many of your conflicts, emotions, and problems by/while listening to my music – especially RD&M [title purposely withheld] which was a total, total bummer – it does get one *right* in the mood – no questions asked.

But, I am digressing.

I came to you today piggybacking on depression and how it relates to success, and I am so grateful for this outlet because, why sure, others have attempted to coax me out of myself since I have crossed over – (I guess that's what you would call it. I actually call it taking up a new residency – a newer, lighter form of being).

And Lord knows I am quite familiar with lightness of being – after all, my addiction brought me to a very lightness of being – ninety six pounds. Imagine.

I think on some level I was doing my utmost best to totally disappear, and I thought, felt, believed on some other level I could do just that.

No one prepares you for overnight success, so on the topic of success, I say take heed. Craft your idea of success and stage it so it does not overwhelm you.

Overnight success is similar to having a ton of bricks fall on you.

It takes your breath away.

It robs you of your identity.

It makes you want to flee from yourself.

At least it did for me.

And I can only speak for myself.

Success had its high points – sitting in the lap of luxury – but going from just getting by to having all you could ever have imagined, plus some, is overwhelming.

It is too much.

It can destroy you.

It destroyed me.

It complicates life.

So plan your success.

Anyone and everyone is capable of achieving success – whatever that looks like for you – just do it as they say, "one day at a time."

My best advice, speaking from experience, is to achieve success in steps.

Plan it out – craft a success plan in incremental steps.

Allow yourself the time and space to take it in and digest it before you move up or on to your next plateau.

It is all about adjusting.

Do not go into overwhelm.

It will take your breath away and might even cause you to take your life away. (Never on purpose, of course, but merely as a means of disappearing from overwhelm.)

I will be back.

This has been an incredible outlet for me – I feel so expressive.

I may even sing again.

Thank you.

[Anonymous]

[This soft, inquisitive, feminine energy came through with a pureness of intention and although she wants to remain anonymous at this time, did add "I am one of everyone". She reserves the right to return and contribute again.]

* ♪ Lyrics have been changed to avoid copyright infringements.

Day 50

You don't know me, but I have heard others mention this 'project' you are working on, and I would like to contribute.

You may refer to me as Sister Spark, Sistress of the free and floating.

I came in on a wave of luscious light and will transform your wildest imaginings.

First, allow me to say *thank you* for trusting me, though I did sense some apprehension on your part when I drifted in from your right – over your shoulder on hues of sea green and turquoise blue.

Thank you for trusting yourself and moving out of your own way – rather quickly, I might add. I sit at your right and have flowed in and out of your energy field for quite some time but have never connected, at least not like this.

I have been carefully watching over you and decided tonight is an ideal time to touch down and land, so to speak.

We are sisters – kindred souls – sistresses – remarkable and magical.

I am pleased to hear you trust us, the free-floating fire bearers, bearing light and sparkles.

Yes, light and sparkles with love and levity.

We have been doing this for ages – I am pleased you are turning to us and seeking our wisdom and guidance.

You are revealing your confidence in your own wisdom by allowing us to guide.

I am pleased that you seek success stories or 'secrets' as you sometimes refer to them – (your project as); although I do believe you know they are not secrets – just stories waiting to be told and shared.

And I am pleased that you have reached this level of confidence and trust in yourself and in others.

This is good.

This reflects progress.

As for sharing stories of success – I do believe if you were to craft your own stories, you will find you have many to share.

You have successfully achieved quite a number of milestones in your young life, but we are not here for that right at this moment.

A successful individual is one who allows themselves to be free floating, unencumbered by unhealthy or toxic thoughts, words, deeds, interactions, one who rises above pettiness and comparison.

One who stands on their own two feet – or flies freely with their own two wings (tee hee) – without a second thought as to what they don't have, possess, or need.

One who finds and feels love at every turn, every waking moment.

One who shares that love with all beings every minute of every hour of every day.

Success is a compassionate soul.

Success is lightness of being, caring for others without regard for one's own needs.

Success is transforming negativity into positivity each and every day.

It is a simple process, by the way.

Do not dwell on success.

Dwell instead on lightness of being and love, and through and in that you will feel and find much more than simply success.

[Sister Spark]

[Although Sister Spark and I have never 'formally' met one another, we do know one another, and we revel in that knowingness.]

Day 49

I'm new at this, and I have kept quiet for pretty much all of my life – so if I appear to be meek, please bear with me.

I appreciate this opportunity to voice my...

[He is apprehensive, pulling his energy back, wondering if he will be 'punished' or if his life will be made more miserable by divulging. I find this most interesting to learn he is experiencing fear and thus not completely free to express himself, – even as his new formless self. Yet he musters up the courage to continue to speak.]

Not much has changed for me.

I am still looking over my shoulder as I speak, fearing recrimination for bearing my soul.

I don't want to make waves nor single myself out – draw attention to my opinions.

I have always chosen to fade into the background, even at the risk of giving up both my manhood and identity.

Humor, smiling, nodding my head in agreement was the method I used to get along, get by, exist.

I am learning new methods, and there are plenty of gentle methods available – but they all feel too out of reach for me.

It's taken me some time to get a handle on being here. In this form.

While it all feels pretty much the same, it all feels so different.

I know anything is possible. It feels much lighter, airier, and breezier here, but I am still heavy with behaviors and thoughts of being on your 'side', the side of the living.

So I try.

I do my best.

I want to feel what others are feeling.

I must continue to do the work.

I am so heavy and so light.

Diametrically opposed.

I am learning so much more about my wife – issues and feelings I never knew she experienced in her life in form.

We live a formless life now.

So I imagine that would be considered a success, I suppose.

We cannot go backward in time. No one has created that option yet – at least not that I'm aware of – so we continue to go forward and learn from our shortcomings and mistakes, wrong turns, unspoken words, silence, complacency.

Not success. Cowardice.

If I were to do it all over again – if I were to shoot for, aim for, plan for a successful life – I would first and foremost be myself.

Speak for myself.

Use my own mind.

Live a life of love but without compromising who I am and what I believe in for the fear of rocking the boat.

I never realized that by me kowtowing to my wife I was hurting – not helping her.

I enabled, or, rather, molded – her into someone she didn't want to be.

I gave in, which made her appear to be someone she wasn't.

It caused her to choose a role for which she was unfit. In doing so, she took the wrong path, which led to a life of misery and unhappiness.

It is important we remain true to ourselves – no matter what. No matter what the cost.

And it is important to talk, have conversations.

Discuss.

Compromise is not a sign of weakness but rather a sign of strength.

But kowtowing – that's just plain weak, wishy-washy, emasculating.

I wish I could have acted on that – then.

I knew this in my heart, but did nothing to stop it. I was afraid.

Instead, I smiled, kept the peace, gave up a piece of myself, and moved along.

You must be able to be comfortable with yourself and your principles.

Speak from your heart and be flexible but strong.

Know when to give in and when to stay strong.

You may not see it in the moment, but oftentimes you will help your wife or husband or the other person become an even stronger and true-to-themselves individual.

Success is not only about money. I achieved all that – a successful business and a great amount of money. I lost all of that too, because I lost myself in the process.

I never learned to say no.

Nor did I ever truly speak my mind.

Don't make the same mistakes.

Know who you are.

Know what you are willing to compromise and how far your boundaries can stretch before you reach the risk of being less than who you aim to become.

Above all – love yourself first.

I must be learning something 'up' here – I never spoke of love before, not in this way.

Something must be sinking in after all.

Yes – you must come first.

And there is a way you can be first along with those you love – your wife, family, friends. I know there is a way, and I know "you" can figure it out.

I can always help.

I am learning – yes, I am. And you are helping me to realize that by simply listening and allowing me to share my story.

Thank you. I love you.

[Anonymous]

[This male energy, near and dear to my heart, came through feeling weak and unexpressed and left feeling centered, balanced, and expressed. Very loving energy – he always has been. He prefers I not mention his name, not at this point. Consider it done. I am happy for him that he was able to share.]

Day 48

We southern women never thought much about success while we were growing up in lack and near poverty.

But we always had hope in our hearts.

We had faith and belief too, and that sustained us during the worst of times and exalted us during the best of times.

I knew I was born to sing and praise the Lord through song. So I held onto that belief and allowed it to feed my soul and even my belly at times.

It – my song, my music, my belief – sustained me and my family.

My mother was a hard worker, and she loved us as hard and as strong as she worked. She cared for all seven of us when times were good and when times were not so good.

But we had our faith and we held on.

Success found me.

I was never looking for it.

I never looked for it.

I just did what came naturally for me...praise the Lord through song.

And I loved to sing the honky-tonk songs, too.

My 'getup' was who I was. Who I was in my soul. I loved my getup. And I loved to sing.

So success found me – Imagine that – being found by success and not looking for it! I never looked for it. I sang.

I suppose, in a way, I attracted success by knowing deep down in my soul my heart's desire.

At a very young age I knew I wanted to sing to express myself – to praise the Lord in song. I would picture myself singing – anywhere and everywhere.

And when at a young age my uncle placed the guitar in my hands, I knew I had come home. It was instant love – both ways. I loved the instrument and the guitar loved me. Perfect companionship. It opened a whole new world for me.

We made music together, and we deeply loved one another, my guitar and me. The more I gave, the more it gave – a sublime exchange.

About the success thing – attraction, I suppose – the one thing I did was to hold tight to any dream of singing on stage and sharing my love and my gift with the world.

Success had her eye on me and quietly coveted my music. Success knew in her heart of hearts that one day she would touch down and light upon me.

Again – I did not know she was watching.

I kept on doing what I was doing and what I loved to do and enjoyed every single solitary moment.

Music flowed through me and my guitar.

The more I wrote and played, the easier it was to write and play more.

See how this works?

So I got myself into a flow, a groove, and I went with it.

No questions asked.

All the while success was watching and she must have been approving, because she hung in there with me. My momma was so proud, and as the money rolled in, her life improved.

But it wasn't about the money for her – it was about her baby daughter doing what she loved – making music and praising the Lord. We were faith-filled people, you know.

So that's an interesting twist on success – ain't it?

If you follow your calling, your heart's desire, and knowing (your soul knows what to do), success will be there to watch over you until the day she touches down and lights upon you.

[Patsy Cline]

[This female country-western performer's candle was blown out very early on in her career. Though her life may have ended, her spirit remains strong and faith filled. Her desire to share her simply stated perspective rang through loud and clear and was replete with determination and love – determination to follow her heart's calling and love for praising the Lord while making her mamma's life just a little easier.

After a car accident in 1961, Patsy Cline was quoted to have said to her mother, "You don't appreciate home until you leave it, and, let me tell you, you can't appreciate life till you've almost left it! Some people hope and die with their song still in them. I used to think that happiness resulted when my earnings matched my yearnings! But not anymore! " She was also quoted to have said, "I don't wanna get rich – just live good."]

Day 47

Success to me was a full heart.

It was complete and unconditional love.

Love without struggle.

We struggled to be loved and to love out loud – not behind closed doors or down dark alleys.

We were a feisty generation expressing our needs and living out loud – as much as we could.

But we were also full of fear.

Fear of the unknown – fear of the known.

It wasn't enough to hold down a good job, pave your way, live an honest life – surrounded by family – a family you loved and who loved you.

While that may have been defined as the stereotypical success story, the underlying message or underlying reality was we weren't successful because we lived in the proverbial closet.

Always looking over our shoulders and wanting more than anything, *including life itself*, to fit in – to belong – to be accepted.

We were crazy kids in a candy store. When we were together – with our own – dancing to the beat of a different drummer – we felt loved. We felt connected and safe and successful. Successful because we had created a community into which we could slip away and simply be.

Simply love.

We didn't have to lie or compromise our integrity. That was so much work. It took a lot of effort to hide – always hide.

Hide in plain sight.

That was the antithesis of success. That was sorrow.

We went crazy; we couldn't get enough. We were like children starving for something to feed us, make us feel whole – but mostly – make us feel okay. Like it was okay to be ourselves.

We devoured that feeling when we were together in community – whether on the dance floor, at the Boat Slip, or gathered at a friend's house doing what we did the best, love.

It was so hard to love and to have an honest love.

It kept us diminished – made us smaller than we really were. It kept us on guard and always fearful.

So success, full-out loud success – was never possible.

Oh, sure, we held the belief that someday things would change, and we had mantras like, "We've come a long way, baby," but for those of us who lived through the seventies and eighties it was nowhere near enough.

Too little, too late.

I found success – true love, but I had to move clear across the country to make that happen.

The last few years of my life were blessed: a loving partner, Dan – someone with whom I could walk side by side in the sunshine without looking over my shoulder.

But I also had to witness his slow death and then, bear witness to my own.

I still don't understand why so many of us died.

I don't get it.

And I hope someday I will – although we don't talk about those types of things here. I can feel a resentment or bitterness deep within about that period of time – the epidemic, which took so many of us.

[Ronnie Umile]

[Ronnie, my dear, dear friend and partner in self-discovery, and I walked side by side, cloaked in secrets and lies as we lived and loved beyond measure. And danced! Oh, did we dance – we danced to celebrate our uniqueness, and we danced to forget our suppression and our sorrow. We partied as if each day was our first, and we partied as if each day was our last. We were out of our minds when gathered together in community, for we knew we were understood and loved for who we were. Nothing more, nothing

less. I have learned from co-counseling with spirit that self-expression is not only necessary but healthy. Though his bitterness comes through loud and clear, my friend is simply processing and purging his feelings so he may be made new once again. Dance on, my disco king, dance on.]

Day 46

Success is like baking a cake – first you need all the right ingredients.

[Julia Child]

[What an honor to have a master chef and teacher pop in to share a simple recipe.]

Success is being able to see things differently through new lenses.

Success is being able to change your point of view.

It's never too late to change your point of view – even if it takes crossing over and seeing things differently.

I must be reaching some pinnacle of success. Since I have been in this new form, I have seen – or, rather, have been able to see – things, life, past life, events, situations – with clearer vision.

I have traveled much and covered a lot of ground since arriving here. I wasn't happy when I first arrived. As a matter of fact, I was living in dread, remorse, and weariness.

All of those 'things' I wanted to achieve – like kindness, compassion, and a deeper sense of love – they were all snatched from me. Or so I thought. Or so I imagined.

I awoke feeling as if all my time had finally – or at long last – run out.

All my options removed from the table.

All the things I wanted to achieve or demonstrate were no longer possible.

I missed my window of opportunity. Yes, the window had closed.

I felt depressed and like a failure. I had failed my husband, I had failed my children, but most of all I had failed myself.

I blew it.

The window had closed, and there was no going back.

I was curt at times during my life on the other side, the earth plane.

I failed to give or demonstrate my love for my husband and especially my children.

I held back on praise – not because I wanted to, but because it felt uncomfortable to do so.

Too much sugar would make them weak – rot their teeth.

I was, and still am, proud of my children and happy for them; although I still hope and pray my eldest son finds a mate soon. No one deserves to be alone, despite being a bitter pill to swallow. He's more like me than he will ever acknowledge.

Mine was not the easiest of childhoods, and what I didn't know was that my upbringing would take a toll on my marriage and my children's lives and how they value themselves.

Besides, somehow, someone planted a bitter, bitter seed deep within me. And while I never knew it had been planted (for a long, long time), when I realized it had sprouted into a bitter, bitter plant within, I knew nothing about how to dig it up – get rid of it – address it.

So I continued feeding it, and it grew stronger, its roots intertwining throughout my heart. It was as if this nasty plant had taken complete hold of my heart.

I did have compassion – a great deal of it – ask the cats – my cats – all the cats. It was *so easy* to be compassionate to the cats. They didn't judge me. They simply loved me.

It was much harder being compassionate to humans – although I am beginning to see I had created that story to allow myself to continue feeding that nasty plant.

My life was taken much too short – snatched from me before I had the chance to change and truly express my deepest feelings.

However, there is a part of me that believes I never could have accomplished that; I never could have changed while I was on "that side".

It has taken me quite some time (although time is irrelevant now) to see – truly see – with new eyes – how I behaved.

How I was powerless to change.

Sort of like Ebenezer Scrooge – he had to return to past lives and be shown the error of his ways. He was lucky; he then had options to exercise when he returned from his travels back in time.

I am beginning to see and learn – especially through my good friend – your mother – that I too have options, and so therefore, I am a success.

I have options, and I recently began to exercise those/my options.

I can still become a true success, and I can certainly help others – especially my daughter – become what is in her heart. I realize now, more than ever, I can do that from my new vantage point here in the afterlife.

While I have made amends to my husband, and we are learning how to "be" in a different way together – I have the power to help others achieve all – or at least some – of what I wasn't able to achieve.

I guess one would call that success.

[Louise R.]

[While I am grateful for Louise's newfound awareness and depth of understanding, and while I marvel over not only the messages and stories the spirits share, it is the insight as to where they are and what is possible from within that realm that I find refreshingly hopeful and encouraging. The possibility of continued growth and self-blossoming feeds my soul.

What I am sensing is it's all about being complete when your life is complete. What you do is not nearly as important as how you feel about yourself.

Who versus Do.

*Instead of focusing on what you do, focus on who you are. Be **who** you are – that's success. Louise now knows she can effectuate change and that's success!]*

Day 45

All right, I'll step out and speak my piece if you're looking for someone to talk; although I'm not sure I have too much to say. But you do know I like to share – although, at times, I find myself to be shy and just need a little egging on, and since there are not too many at this stage (or so it feels) wanting to step up – I will.

I can sense [the energy of] others milling about and can sense their timidness – not knowing what to make of all this – but knowing something is definitely going on.

For me it's all about fun and having a laugh and getting out and enjoying yourself no matter what else is going on or has taken place in your life.

So we all lose our spouses – get over it. And I'm not saying that to be wise, but what's the sense of being depressed about all that? We know someone has to go – so count your blessings if you get to stay a little while longer.

Any cause for a celebration is all right with me.

I can't say I feel comfortable using the word "success," but I am comfortable with the word "happy"– happy-go-lucky.

Involved.

Moving.

In motion.

Friends are important, and my friends made me feel like a queen.

I always felt rich like a queen when I was out and about with my friends, because I don't believe anyone should be alone. It's not good for you. It dampens your spirits.

Wealthy in friendship, I suppose, would be success. And making people laugh and feel good is always something that made me feel good, so I suppose that's successful.

And laugh – I loved to laugh. I still do my share of laughing and singing; it just feels a little different.

I can't pinpoint it.

It's almost as if I kept myself busy and laughing as a way of coping, and now it feels like it's just who I am.

Natural.

An everyday occurrence.

In my bones.

In my blood.

Most of all – the most important part of living a successful life is to love and to be loved.

Even after your spouse is gone – even after losing my husband – I always knew I was loved and I loved him and that kept me going.

It's important to have fun – even when times seem dark and dismal and hard to go on – enjoy whatever bit of happiness you can find.

And look for it because it's there; you can always find something to be happy about or something to make someone laugh about, and that feels good. So I suppose if you think about it – that's success.

And don't ever, ever give up or give in.

Persevere – that's the mark of a truly successful person.

Don't give in and stay happy.

[Ellen Boyle]

[My godmother, the woman who, at the time of my birth, suggested I be named Iowna – was a hot ticket from the word "go". She knew how to bring light, levity, and laughter to any situation and lived her life to its fullest. How wonderful to hear her effervescent spirit still going strong as she shares her love and lightness of being.]

Day 44

A new month, a new beginning, and hope springs eternal.

Today marks the forty-fourth day of this, our endeavor.

Forty-four was your age when I crossed over.

What does the number forty-four represent? You may be interested to find out.

The word "charmed" comes to mind.

I know you are focusing on others when you invoke questions about success, and I also know success is defined by each person's unique experience, longing, and desires.

I want to focus on you for a minute and let you know I have always considered you to be a success.

You have a way with people.

You bring out the best in others.

You are kind, compassionate, and very, very loving.

I have always known this although I didn't tell you often enough.

I communicate my feelings in nonverbal ways, but I don't believe you ever received the full impact of my desires.

I want you to know at this highly pivotal time in your life that I am and always have been proud of you – but most importantly – proud of what you have accomplished up until now.

It was no easy feat to conquer your devils – give the devil its due – but you did it. And I was there with you. I saw what that took for you to stop drinking,

I never told you enough how proud of you I was.

I don't want to go off track (and this probably isn't the time or place), but I saw the number forty-four, and it triggered something within me.

It takes a lot of courage to follow your dreams – especially when your back is against the wall, and you doubt your own gifts and abilities.

But I want you to know that you are successful. You have always been successful, and you have always accomplished anything you put your mind to.

There's the secret to success – anything you put your mind to.

If you think back – and you may want to – to those times in your life when everything just flowed, and you felt really good (despite your challenges, battles, or the secrets you kept hidden away) – those times were the times you stuck to it – you put your mind to it, and didn't let up.

You were a willful child; and you still are a willful child.

I guess I popped in here today to pick you up and brush you off, to give you a pat on the back, and remind you that when you put your mind to something there's no stopping you.

Don't look outside of yourself for success.

(I do love this project – that's not what I'm referring to), just connect with that deepest part of you on a more regular basis.

That deep part where your true success resides.

You are a successful woman.

You were born successful.

Don't, please don't, ever forget that or lose sight of that.

[Leah 'Ma' Ford]

[I contemplated whether or not I would include this personal message from my mother, Leah. I decided if she mustered up the energy to pay a visit, she must have felt it imperative to have her message shared. While the message is personal in nature, it is also universal and delivers with it the promise of support and love from above. We are never really alone or devoid of encouragement.

By the way, I looked up the number forty-four in Doreen Virtue's book Angel Numbers 101. Are you ready for the explanation? "The angels are giving you extra comfort, love, and support right now. Ask them for help with everything, and listen to their guidance through your intuition."

Spot on, Ma. Spot on!]

Day 43

Success is getting up each morning, putting your pants on one leg at a time, and going "out there" one step at a time.

Never despairing – no matter what.

I always considered myself a successful man because I knew what I knew. Wise beyond my years and passionate, extremely passionate.

For me, my success began at a very young age. I was born and raised to believe in the American dream – where anything and everything was possible. And I had dreams – big dreams.

As a Seabee I was very good with my hands and my mind.

I traveled the world and felt hopeful and successful.

I never looked at my life or the world as something I could not have – meaning I always saw the glass as being half full and, most of the time – all full – totally full.

It begins in your heart.

For me the feeling was always in my heart.

Anything and everything was possible. Still is. The world is your oyster.

I never, ever, ever gave up.

I always believed in the good of mankind despite having to deal with some buggers in my life. Less than honest men.

I walked a fine line between maintaining my honesty and keeping my job.

People wanted me to lie, cheat, steal, pad my accounts, slip them a little something on the side. But I held fast to my integrity and beliefs. I couldn't keep jobs because I wouldn't play with the "big boys"– I wouldn't get into bed with the sharks.

My family didn't know this. Why would I burden them with that? Besides, my wife was experiencing her own unique set of challenges.

It became a game for me. How far could I go keeping my values and being honest in a world – rather, on a playing field – that, while they expected your best work, they preyed upon your worst values.

They wanted to see how low you could go.

Tempting, to say the least – but not my bag.

My parents taught me I could achieve anything through hard work and honesty.

The value of success is measured...
by a man's (or woman's) sense of values.

An honest man is a successful man.

A man who is loved by his family and children is a successful man.

A man who never, ever stops trying to be his best – to go out there every day and be his best – is a successful man.

And a man who is loved and admired by his children long after he leaves this earth is a successful man.

[Al R.]

[A hard-working, highly ethical "fella" who stopped in to share his point of view. Though I am closely connected and happen to know his essence well enough, I honor his need to withhold his full identity and simply acknowledge his vulnerability and honesty. Thank you, Al.]

Day 42

She who masters her time is truly a successful woman.

We all feel like we have an unlimited, inexhaustible, bottomless pit of time available to us, and so we do what we please whenever we please with little or no attention given to time.

Time runs out.

Time, in the literal sense, on a linear plane.

I, too, once believed I had all the time in the world. Time to lollygag, time to decide, always plenty of time to decide and those decisions ranged from what shall I eat for dinner to how shall I chose my destiny?

Rule my destiny; live my life.

I was never serious about the serious issues until I had to become serious, and let me tell you girls – serious is not fun, and I am all about making and having fun.

I never gave any though to time – like water drops dripping slowly from a downspout.

Sure I checked my watch or was mindful when I was supposed to be somewhere or meet someone at a certain time.

What I'm referring to is how I used every single precious minute of my life.

I didn't really give a (I want to say a "rat's ass" but will say "care in the world") about precious minutes.

Time lost in indecisions.

Time wasted in the middle of thoughts.

Indecisions and indecisiveness are two of the biggest areas of lost time.

I equate it to burning money.

Think about that for a moment, if you will.

Take a dollar bill, hold a match to it, and watch it burn until ultimately you have a small stack of ashes.

That, for me, epitomizes wasted time.

You'll never get that dollar bill back.

Precisely.

Nor will you get that time back

I'm here to tell you first hand – you will never get time back, nor will you be able to stop time, increase time, or change time.

You must make the best and most of every minute you have.

On some level it's exhilarating creating a bucket list and doing your best to cram in everything you've ever imagined doing into a short window of time.

Sure, it gets your blood pumping and is a great exercise of focus, determination, and fortitude – but quite frankly, it sucks.

If you think about all the perceived time you have RIGHT NOW – to create and execute a bucket list – or a list of your biggest, wildest dreams – you could take a deep breath and plan.

But you must execute, and you must get over the notion or idea that you can do it tomorrow.

For some of us, tomorrow never comes.

I'm sorry for being so *candid* – but I'm speaking firsthand and doing my best to spare you the sorrow of unfulfilled moments…dreams… ideas.

Call that friend.

Make your vision board.

Create your dreams.

Write your bucket list. (You may want to change the name to something more appealing than "bucket list.")

Be the change you want to see.

Love now.

Be bold.

Go where no one has dared to tread.

Live loud.

Laugh often.

Love much.

And do it now.

Do it always.

True success is eking out every single inch or centimeter of life in the moment.

Remember – now is all we have.

We don't get do-overs.

We don't get a return on our time if we don't like how it feels, fits, or works – (or doesn't work).

You can't bring it back; ask for a refund or exchange.

It's real.

It's now.

It's yours to do with whatever you choose.

Choose wisely – choose now – and live now!

[Candace Hopkins]

[Candid Candace coming through in spirit as she did in form – loving, expressive, and straight forward. Candace does not mince her words and always tells it like it is. I value her counsel and giggle right alongside of her. Light as a feather and profound as the day is long. Keep them coming, Candace. Keep them coming!]

Day 41

Now is the time for all good women to step up, step forward, carry the lanterns of light, and initiate change.

We are a collective of women from past generations who have bound together to bring forth the light.

We are gathering en masse to assist through this dark period.

It is NOT as dark as the darkness of past – and it holds great possibility and hope, but we must march – we are marching, and we know we will make a difference.

The question is – will you?

It is not the time for apathy or laziness. It is a time of great awakening and change.

There are many of us gathering and gaining great momentum.

We have a cause, and it includes you.

We speak of success as survival plus some.

Survival is a basic instinct. Anything and everything above that basic instinct we term as success.

Actually to survive is to be successful.

There are many who did not survive or who are barely surviving.

But lest we not demean them nor refer to them as unsuccessful – for try as they might, they failed – were opposed, beaten, kept down.

The question then would be, did they really fail – if they died trying?

We think not.

So, success, failure, try as you might, is moot. It's a moot point.

Effort = success.

Anything, any cause one takes up for which they fight or take a stand – is successful.

There are many points of view and interpretations around success and the energy of success.

It is time now to pick up your lantern and go forth in the darkness, shining your light and carrying your message.

That is success.

Getting the message of love, hope, belief.

Belief in all things being possible.

Belief in the power one possesses to create or change.

Belief in a world full of love, grace, and family.

March forth with your head held high – in good spirits and vitality.

You are the bearers of the word, the keepers of the light, the ones this world is depending upon IN THIS MOMENT.

We are here and growing in large numbers, here to help carry the torches and provide support, love, encourage-ment, and strength.

Success. We need another successful wave of awakenings and sisterhood.

We need to save that for which we have worked so diligent-ly and passionately and that for which we lovingly fought to preserve.

Many of us lost our lives in the process – over the years – Joan of Arc and many others too numerous to mention.

We are counting on awakening the sleepy sister everywhere.

Counting on all to step up, step out, and carry the torch and the message of love, belief, faith, and hope.

It is never too late.

Now is the time.

We are with you.

We need you.

We need your voice.

We need your movement.

We need you to get into action.

We need you to be successful now.

[A Collective of Believers]

[This multigenerational collective of believers joined together to bear this message of great import. There is a passion and sense of import in their delivery.]

Day 40

Success is having your eyesight restored.

[Simone… "Black dog, black dog" ♫]

[*Beautiful! Our beloved rescue dog, faithful friend, and Buddy's constant companion, Simone. When she came to live with us, her vision was severely compromised due to cataracts. Within weeks of her adoption, she underwent cataract surgery and lens replacement. We would gaily sing "See Simone See" as we experienced pure joy bearing witness to Simone coming into her vision. How stunning it is that Simone made her way through to share this straight-forward message about success.*]

❖ ❖ ❖

Success is having a full heart, a few bucks in your pocket, and a good woman who loves you.

It's the feeling of having it all – health, wealth, and love. A good job to support you – one you actually enjoy getting up and going to each and every day, with a good retirement plan when your work is through.

It's having a decent roof over your head and a soft bed to rest your head on every night.

It's going to sleep with a full stomach, and though you may have a few cares in the world, you don't really worry because you know they will be taken care of.

It's having a country you believe in and support and even lay your life down for, if need be. It's living in a country in which you feel safe, secure, protected, and free to speak your mind and believe what you'd like.

Having friends and family are signs of a successful man. The frosting on the cake is to have them love you too.

Happiness and contentment are signs of success and a knowing deep within that all is well.

I was raised (by wonderful parents, by the way) to believe that anything is possible.

So to exercise that belief and make anything and all things possible in my lifetime was successful.

Success is going to your grave whether you're ready for it or not – (and in my case, I was not ready) with a knowing that you have accomplished everything you ever wanted to.

[Mac]

[A dear friend of the family and proud World War II veteran; "Mac" – short and sweet.]

Day 39

Success is holding back something for yourself.

A little something for yourself.

I learned that too late.

Actually, I learned that right in time.

I learned it from the best position in which I can share, and that's right here, right now – with you.

And it's good to know I have this opportunity available for me through you and anyone else who cares to listen.

It took me my whole life on the earth plane (I suppose you can call it), and it took me until the here and now to put it into words and make good use of it.

You see, I was the consummate people pleaser. I lived to please others much to my own expense.

It was such a struggle for me because I knew, on some level, it would be the death of me (figuratively – not literally).

I gave, gave, gave until I was on empty – tapped out – and even then I kept giving.

I tapped into my reserve tank, and running on reserve is dangerous to one's well-being.

I gave of my heart; I gave of my soul; I gave of my faith. When someone didn't have enough of something, I gave them some of mine, and even when I didn't have anything or anymore to give, I gave and I gave more.

If I had to borrow to give more – I borrowed.

Boy was that sick.

Although I never saw it that way – except, on some level, I think I did – and I didn't want to confirm that, or else I would have had to stop giving, and I could not have done that.

To stop giving would have been to stop living – to cease to exist.

Tapped out.

Brain cancer.

Nothing left to give.

I gave my all.

Now I know better.

I see differently from where I am.

I am strong, healthy – fully intact – mentally and spiritually, and I have clear, clear vision.

I have remained quiet up until now because I didn't feel as if I had anything of substance or value to contribute.

But I do.

And I do – there are no "buts" about it.

My lesson on success centers on keeping a little something for yourself.

I say "a little" because I know there are a lot of you out there who give as much as I did, and if I were to say keep a lot – it would stop you in your tracks.

So start off with keeping just a little.

A little love – keep some of that for yourself. If you're not able to fully love yourself – you ain't going to be able to fully love someone else.

It's not being selfish.

It's an act of selflessness.

It takes a big act of courage to love yourself.

I couldn't – not fully. So I loved others bigger and better than I loved myself. Especially my husband and my family and my friends.

Jean knows that – she's here with me – we talk about these lessons. As long as we continue to learn.

Keep some time for yourself.

Time – that nonrenewable resource. (I like that term.)

It is imperative to make and keep time for yourself – whatever that looks like for you.

If the thought of that is too overwhelming – start out in small increments…

Ten minutes here, twenty minutes there.

Do the things you always thought about doing but would never make the time to do…

Soak in a tub.

Call a friend.

Read a book.

Relax by the pool.

For God's sake – do something.

Then build upon those steps.

Go ahead – make a list of the little things you can begin to keep for yourself and enjoy yourself.

It needs to be guilt-free, ladies – I *mean* guilt-free.

No taking it back after with the "oh, I never should have _____" (fill in the blank).

Be gentle and good with and to yourself.

Save some for yourself – that's success!

[Nancy W.]

[I know this woman well and can feel her resolve in the sharing of lessons she has learned. Nancy always had a big heart and gave so much of herself to everyone – family, friends, and colleagues. One would say she was generous to a fault. It brings me great joy to know her generous heart now overflows with love of self. Her wisdom is priceless, and her need to share has not lessened a bit. Though she came through loud and clear, she wants to remain partially anonymous.]

Day 38

[Hesitation ... thinking ... how do I start this ...?]

My happy-go-lucky days of youth wound up becoming a "stiff-upper-lip, day-by-day" existence of my adulthood.

You know how happy-go-lucky – bubbly – easygoing I had always been – always looked on the bright side of life.

Even when my stepmother had breast cancer, even though we disagreed a great deal and my father always sided with her, even though Begley broke my heart over and over again – I always maintained a modicum of joy.

Always smiling – I truly believed I could weather any storm as long as I maintained a happy-go-lucky outlook.

And for the most part I did.

Cancer, and the roller coaster ride it unwillingly took me on, kicked the ever-loving daylight out of me. It toyed with and teased me.

It gave me days, weeks, months of reprieve – led me to believe it had abandoned all hope of ever truly getting to me, then turned around when I was less than vigilant – when I allowed joy to return; when I stopped looking for a moment – and knocked me down and reclaimed my life.

It never reclaimed my entire spirit, but it did an awfully good job of giving me a run for my money.

I equate success with luck – although not all lucky people are successful, and not all successful people are lucky.

Some are just better prepared than others.

For me – **a successful day was** a day when I didn't have to think about what cancer was robbing from me.

Any day without a thought to cancer was a good day, a successful day.

For the purpose of my sharing, I say any day that something, *anything*, does not cause you to stray from your life's purpose or distract you from reaching your dreams or goals is a day of success.

I do have something with which I can to tie this all together – and I thought I would come off as a complainer rather than a contributor.

I guess I never got an opportunity to complain about my heartache and battles because I was too busy keeping a stiff upper lip.

I never stopped believing, even when they were shoveling dirt on my grave – so to speak.

I still believe, and I still don't know – why me.

I'm learning.

We're all learning.

We are introspective and retrospective.

We're reflective and meditative.

Our past, while it cannot change, is mutable – can dictate or influence our present – and we certainly are capable of being of service. And that's why I stepped forward after much trepidation – to share my thoughts.

I trust you – I know your intention is pure, and it has been way too long since we've connected. Plus, now that I "hear" myself spilling my guts, I am beginning to feel better about my plight and *where* I am – *who* I am – and *how* I am in this moment.

Believe it or not – memories do keep us alive.

Our memories keep us alive. And those of you who continue to remember and talk about us serve to keep us alive, and that's all we ask for – to be kept alive.

Vital.

Contributing.

A part of.

Connected.

Happy-go-lucky.

Look, I have appeared to come full circle.

Here I was feeling sorry for myself and the agony I, and those who loved me, went through and feeling angry about it all when, in purging myself – I have come to realize that I am still that happy-go-lucky gal who walked in flesh and blood.

How very interesting.

Nothing really changes – except our form.

I have taken on a new form – and *cancer be damned* (you can't touch me now) – but not much else has changed about me. I'm still "Bucko" and still happy-go-lucky.

You have opened a pathway of connection for me – made it a simple process to reach out – made me feel safe, and best of all, allowed – no, you encouraged me to trust myself, you helped me take that courageous first step to connection, and it feels good.

It is so good to be connected to someone who is still connected to the flesh and blood of it all – you get it – you get the pain and anguish, yet you allow us to make the connection while feeling safe to simply be who we are.

You've always had a knack for that, Ford. I love you and appreciate you helping me to reach out. You have opened a whole new world for me, and you have just begun to hear from me and it feels so good.

Thank you.

[Kathleen Buckley]

[I experienced such a roller coaster of emotions as I typed her words; it was as if my friend "Bucko" was sitting right next to me, and we were looking into each other's eyes – a deep, soulful experience. I felt sorrow and sadness for missed opportunities and regretted not being there more for her while she fought the good fight. Thoughts of friends I have been meaning to call – yet "life gets in the way" – crossed my mind.

Thoughts of our happy-go-lucky, teenage days brought a smile to my face. As I typed, my emotions meshed with hers, waxing and waning with every word. What joy to witness her full circle experience and growth. We all need to be loved, to feel connected, and to belong. It matters not what form we take. It matters not the realm in which we dwell. We are all connected, and it is imperative we begin to see and feel that connection – for us, for them. We have so much to learn; they have so much to share. Amazing!]

Day 37

Red velvet.

Hat?

Cushion?

Fluffy.

Smooth.

Soft.

Number fourteen.

Traveled a great distance to get here. No problem. I *love* traveling. From there to here. Interesting proposal. I thought it would take much more of an effort; I was mistaken – it was effortless. But then again, I should have known that, as my travels on the earth plane were effortless and numerous.

Theater delight. The number fourteen – mention that. I am reaching out because she reached out to me, and although you and I have never met, and have never formally nor informally met, nor have we been introduced to one another, we are connected through her.

Please allow me to introduce myself and make that connection now: Tom S. I feel as if I know you on some level, wavelength – energy matrix.

I am glad to be here – to have traveled the distance though distance is immeasurable.

My head is beginning to throb…

Deep exhale.

Pause.

I agreed to come and talk about success – a topic I know well, after creating much of it for myself with little effort, I might add.

[Showing me pyramids, sand. Energy fading in and out.]

I feel dizziness – an inability to focus clearly.

I want to tell you how I feel about success, yet I feel as if I am meeting up with resistance.

Strangely odd.

I am usually off and running, so I will attempt to compose myself and push through this for the sake of completing my mission. I did say I would attempt to connect...

No, actually, I said I would make a connection.

Following your heart's calling is the building block of success.

It begins with a calling – it ends – strike that, – as it never ends – not really.

So, it begins with a calling – a desire.

Oftentimes we – the collective – "we"– brush that aside – that calling, our calling – as it may feel too insurmountable or out of the question.

If you keep returning to that one single thought, then you must obey its command. Resistance is futile, so don't fight the feeling.

Allow yourself to go with the flow – that would be key #2,

Key #1 is listen to your calling.

Key #2 is allow yourself to go with the flow.

As soon, or shortly thereafter, as you let go – the real magic begins. Don't question it – don't sabotage yourself with questions. Follow the natural progression as unnatural as it may seem or feel.

Key #3 – allow the magic to happen – don't sabotage yourself with questions.

Sometimes that which feels so unnatural is the natural course of action – only feeling unnatural because you have never let yourself go to feel it.

Feel your feelings.

Feel the excitement.

Get in touch with and in tune with the possibilities.

They are unlimited – you get to choose.

Key #4 – Yep, you've got it – feel your way to unlimited possibilities. You are the master or mistress of your journey.

The heavens will open for you – not in the literal sense – all doors will open for you.

It's as if you board the vessel of your heart's desire – your feelings, coupled with the actions you take, inspired by your feelings will help you create your heart's desire – help you to bring to fruition your wildest desires – and in doing so, you create your own success.

It's really a very simple formula, but it takes dedication and belief.

Key #5 then is to enjoy yourself upon your arrival. You will get there if you choose to.

You will achieve your wildest successes if you listen to and follow your heart,

I did, and I am – still!

I'll be back.

This was fun.

And good.

Very good.

[Thomas Scalise]

[We've all heard the expression "six degrees of separation," which is the theory "that everyone and everything is six or fewer steps away, by way of introduction, from any other person in the world, so that a chain of a-friend-of-a-friend statements can be made to connect any two people in a maximum of six steps. (http://en.wikipedia.org/wiki/Six_degrees_of_separation)."

There are two degrees of separation between Tom and me. I recognized his energy when he began to talk about his love for traveling. Then he "showed" me the pyramids. I remembered seeing a postcard from Egypt, which he had sent to my partner a few years back. I am touched he chose to contribute. Thanks, Thomas.]

Day 36

Kate so infrequently asks for anything – when I heard her call for help, I knew I had to be there – show up – be present.

I appreciate you, Diane, trusting me and believing in me.

As I said, Kate so infrequently reaches out – it was so good to make the connection. Johnny-on-the-spot – that's me!

And you need not do anything except continue to be attentive you, with an open channel, open heart, and willingness and eagerness to pen my words.

Thank you.

Success begins with a full heart.

Let me rephrase that – Success is a full heart.

Success is living life on purpose.

Coming out of all closets, and we know what that entails, girls, now don't we?

I'm not referring to the proverbial gay closet, in which we had (well, most of us had) lived for years – but all closets. Closets of denial; "not good enough"; "cannot possibly do that"; "who me?"; "hardly!" or self-deprecation.

All it takes is one misspoken word or comment, and we are off and running back to our safe space – that quiet darkness – with the door safely slamming behind us. Yet after a while it becomes too dark and claustrophobic. Easy to run there – escape to – not so easy to remain there for any real length of time. Certainly not enough to make a statement – and it's all about making statements.

So why bother?

I say come out and stay out.

Stay out and shine your light.

That's success.

Success is believing – really believing – in yourself on a deeper level. The deepness which you feel in your heart and soul.

Many of us have felt that – I think I believe you know what I'm referring to. I guess you might call it passion. Your passion place.

The light and the spark. As soon as you spark the belief and shine your light there is no going back and nothing can erase nor take away your belief. It's yours to keep forever and ever and then some.

Why… I still believe!

Imagine that!

And why wouldn't I?

I was fully out.

My light was bright – And – so I believed.

It may have been a long time coming, but girls, when you've got it – you've got it.

Success isn't something you strive for – it's not something you write/list at the top of your to-do list, "I want success." – It's something you live.

It's a feeling.

It's a light within.

It is cultivated and it is nurtured by your faith and belief.

When I say it's a feeling – I mean it's a *feeling*.

Just imagine what FEELING SUCCESSFUL might *feel* like.

Close your eyes, and try it on for a fit. *Feel* it everywhere.

Imagine and then put it into action as whatever you need to do to create the feeling.

But don't push it – don't try. It's more about release, letting go, and allowing the feeling to find you and permeate throughout every cell in your body.

What if I were to tell you the secret of being successful or the secret of success has nothing to do with finding or making success – and everything to do with loving and nurturing yourself – living your passion, and loving life each and every day – and by doing that, success will find you?

Would you believe me?

Now there's something to ponder.

That wasn't that bad, Diane now was it? We'll have to do this again sometime.

Love to Kate.

['Herkie' Wingfield]

[Herkie, another "six degrees of separation" encounter. Though I have never officially met Herkie, I feel as though I know him through the colorful and heartfelt stories shared by Katharine as she relived her days in San Francisco. Again, I am touched and honored that Herkie cared enough to muster up the energy and share. Thanks, Herkie.]

Day 35

One woman's success is another woman's mess.

Now ain't that the truth?

'Cause I certainly made a mess out of my success.

I turned my success into a big mess.

[Strumming, strumming to the tune of "Me and Bobby McGee" ♫ singing, "I made a mess of my success." ♪]

I overdid everything.

I lived larger than my body and spirit could hold or contain.

Contain – that's more like it – my spirit couldn't contain my energy – can you believe that? I was too large for my container.

My container couldn't contain me.

That's the makings for a cool song.

My container couldn't contain me.

You get my drift? Sometimes someone comes along who is too big for themselves – their spark ignites, and – *poof!* – they burn out as quickly as the spark went to flame.

That's success too quickly. Or is it too much energy in too small of a place?

I'm not quite sure.

I'm still making music.

There's lots of us here still making and playing music.

So it's not all that bad.

Hard, heavy, rock.

Nearly killed me.

Wait, no, it did kill me. *[Laughs]*

[I love this laugh – guttural, raspy, genuine.]

So… success was short-lived.

Let me tell you a little about it – what a time – what a time in the history of America. We were all in an uproar – protesting. We were growing faster than the energy – form – could accommodate.

We came into an awareness that was much bigger than us. As a people we had been held down for far too long – unable to express ourselves – lacking the words and the opportunity, we basically walked around numb, and we accepted this numbness as normal.

That is until everything changed.

It was as if a wave of consciousness filled with awareness swept over us. Those who were attuned to this – got it – (sort of like what is taking place *right now.*)

When we got it – it startled us awake – we knew there was "a change a comin'" and we knew *we* were the change.

This wave of change and consciousness and awareness bathed us in courage and in an inability to step back – to retreat to whence we had been was not an option.

Forward.

We created a forward movement through music. The lyrics were simple yet full of messages – inspiring people to rise up and join us. Our music awoke the savage beast – or, rather, the love beast.

Since we were existing in a state of sublime numbness, we had become an America of apathy.

Our music and our presence tapped into the love within us all, and when love was reawakened, people began to see differently, love more deeply, and crave more justice.

Boy, did we ignite change. It was all very serious – our mission to awaken – yet it was all very playful. We partied just as hard and fast as we loved and moved forward. We had a mission – the mission had chosen us – simply because we had become attuned to the possibility of "more than just this," and we threw our entire selves into this mission.

Totally.

That was success. We were successful. We initiated and maintained a serious shift in consciousness – and America has never been the same. Thank God. We needed that. It has changed the world.

Hundreds, thousands, millions of young adults stepped forward, got it, felt it, and joined us. We created a new world. We brought a much-forgotten – hardly ever discussed, greatly needed emotion and feeling out into the forefront and shared with the planet, really. Love.

Love was and still is our tenet.

Don't you forget this, please?

We did it all for love.

And justice.

And attention to the plight of this world.

Yet in our enthusiasm and fueled by our passion (and being one of many who were too big for their containers – too much energy for form) – we burnt ourselves out.

We extinguished our own flame.

We went down with a big bang.

So my big tip for success – or what I would like to pass along is – take it slow.

Incremental success is the best success.

Slow and steady.

Easily digestible.

Some of us are too much energy for our spirits – you don't need to let that burn you out anymore.

That I have learned from this, the other side, which is not really as you call the other side – we are very much with you on your side – we are simply in another form – free floating, transparent, energy without matter.

I always chuckle when I hear you all refer to the other side.

Man, that's separateness at its finest.

We are all one, and we all cohabitate together.

It is not the other side – it is this side without form.

If you need something sexy sounding, then let's do it – let's create it. Hell, I'll even create a song. Write and sing it just for you, Diane.

So for those of you who are too much energy – and you know who you are (hint, hint) – take it slow – but don't take it so slow that you're motionless.

Success is a perfect blend of slow motion with action. Like walking a tightrope

You must keep walking – moving forward – get out there and make your statement.

Awaken the world – (begin with your little corner), share your message, and take small bites. Integrate them. Don't allow your passion to cause you to burn yourself out.

Too much too soon won't do it.

I think you get my message, which is "one woman's success is another woman's mess."

I made a mess of my success because I didn't have the wherewithal to contain my energy. No, I didn't have the wherewithal or foresight, maybe the patience also.

I was so fired up – but I didn't have the knowing to pace myself, and I – through my passion and crazy ways and over excessiveness – burnt myself out. Made a mess of my success.

So pace yourself, and go out there – spread the word, there is "a change a comin'" (again). Don't put the metal to the petal, take it slow and easy.

But do not, under any terms, give up or fall back into apathy.

Rise now

And be

Your successful you.

I'll be strumming, and I will be back with something sexy.

We're not on the other side.

Blended?

[Janis Joplin]

[This feminine energy made herself known from the get-go. She was pushy, gruff, and passionate about being heard and sharing her message. Her love resonated in every word she spoke. She wanted to make sure she shared her experience around success so that others could learn and acquire their success differently. It was an honor to banter with Janis Joplin and hold the space as she rambled on with clarity, compassion and a sense of purpose. Wowza!]

Day 34

What is all this fuss about success?

I just don't get it.

What good is success if you're not happy?

I guess happiness is the key to success; actually happiness is far greater than success.

You can keep your success.

Just give me my happiness.

My parents were highly successful, but they weren't very happy. That trickled down – sort of. That was my poison.

Nothing made me happy – not things, not money. I would have taken love – I wish I had been offered more of it.

Love, that is.

I was adrift – lost in nothingness. That was until I found drugs and alcohol. I escaped into them. They helped re-place my longing for love. They were faux love. I didn't need anything else as long as I had them.

Until they had me.

It's a slippery slope.

The crossover.

The turning point.

When you go from having them to them having you.

Then it's all over – a losing battle. As it was for me.

As for success – I would have chosen happiness and love – lots of love. I guess that would be success or a successful person would be someone who is loved – greatly loved – and has a lot of love to give. Genuine love.

I really don't know what that might have felt like.

I know I sound bitter. I'm working on it.

Mostly upset with myself.

Everything was my choice. I made the decisions. Sure, I can blame others – but it really wasn't anyone else's fault but my own. I'm making the best of my current situation, and that's why I am reaching out – partly because I want to soften my edges by helping others, and partly because I needed to.

I needed to make a connection and let you know I am struggling with this sense of bitterness.

I know I will work through it – I see others doing that. I feel light and …

[Unable to express herself.]

Well, let's just say I have good days and not so good days.

I am watching them, my parents, though they don't look too happy, which makes me wonder about the purpose of success.

What purpose did it serve them?

Maybe because they were never really happy to begin with. Who knows?

I have enough on my mind right now.

Yes, I probably should have reached out more – but I was incapable.

I totally surrendered to my sickness.

In part, success is not sickness. You know the kind of sickness I'm talking about.

Self-inflicted.

That's not success.

Success is happiness.

Better yet – strive for happiness, not success – and in doing so you will be successful.

[Anonymous]

[As soon as this feminine energy began to share, I knew exactly who she was, as there is a characteristic that defines her, and it came through loud and clear. She asked that I not identify her, as she does not want her parents to know who she is. Before she transitioned, she drifted aimlessly and constantly fought her demons. Her demons won. I take comfort in the fact that she reached out and connected. She is working through her bitterness and coming to terms with her feelings. She is no longer drifting aimlessly.]

Day 33

Success, Smashing Success!

Do I know a thing or two about success?

Why, yes, I do; I believe I do.

And I am here to share with you.

Waxing poetic.

Charming.

Enough about that.

Invitations – I just love an invitation. All it takes is an invitation plus a desire to accept then the willingness to go.

Accept. Acknowledge. Arrive.

I have arrived and I am pleased to be here.

Success is a funny thing.

Many people speak of success as if it were another appendage – an extension of who they are. As if they were born with a third arm or second head. It is a funny thing – sometimes even a laughing matter – because, after all, who really cares whether you are extremely successful, über-successful, or moderately successful? No one really.

No one except those who are following your every move.

The enemy, the press, the critics.

And, of course, nine out of ten times they're not celebrating your success – they're watching to see if you fail.

Now that's what *they* call a success – your failing.

Do you see what I'm talking about?

Who cares about success?

It's really about how well you execute your craft.

It's all about your performance. How well you perform.

The pressure to be successful in your role may be perceived by others – rather, by the way others perceive you – and you always want to please others and give your best performance – but I have always reserved the right to gauge my own performance, hence monitor my own success.

It's simply that simple.

I am my own best and worst critic.

I determine success with each and every performance on or offstage, in front of or behind a camera. Me, I critique myself.

Success, in my view, from my point of view – is highly personal and serves to improve my craft.

I measure my success by how well I perform.

In retrospect I should have also been measuring my success by how well I treated others.

I wasn't all that nice all the time – too strict on myself – it spilled over at times.

Had I been aware of the necessity of critiquing my behavior as well as my performance, I do believe I would have been far more successful – a far better success.

All we have is now.

So here I am – heeding the call, accepting the invitation, and reaching out at your request.

There is a great deal to learn and share – to continue to learn and share – and I believe if we all strive to learn and share together, we will be a far better success story all-around.

Blimey well.

Richard.

[Sir Richard Harris]

[Sir Richard Harris is a "six degrees of separation" con-nection and feisty spirit, if I do say so myself. Spirit never ceases to amaze me. During the sixty days of my writing this book, a person near and dear to my heart connected

with those she knew and loved (in spirit) and invited them to contribute, if they so chose. Richard accepted the invitation. His energy is infectious and his demeanor, confident and all-knowing. Thank you, Sir Richard.]

Day 32

Honesty is the best policy, *and* if you never tell a lie, you will never have to remember what you said.

You and I met many, many years ago, and I know you have an image of me in your mind that you reflect back upon again and again. (You should really find those photographs and make them visible. My blood is your blood – I am the mother of your father.)

I am reaching out today more so to make a connection but also to remind you that I, too, am here for you. You are my granddaughter, and although we did not have a great deal of time together on the earth plane, does not mean we cannot make up for it now.

I am a touch away.

I am just a touch away.

And I do know a thing or two about running a successful business – I did have an all-around store during trying times in America. Sundries, cigarettes, the basics. It was in the basement of our tenement building, so I, too, worked from my home – just like you.

The key to my successful business (and I refer to it as "my business" and not "your grandfather's and mine" because he was not around much, and then he died at a very young age – you know that story; your father has shared that with you. My husband's death broke your father's heart – but his faith healed it, and he rebounded nicely.

As I was saying – the key to my successful business was generosity. I was born with a generous spirit and always gave willingly with an open heart. Even during the lean years – I shared what little I had.

Extra rooms in my house for weary travelers – a meal or two for someone down on their luck – a pack of cigarettes here, a quart of milk there – on account.

I believed.

I had a strong faith (still do), and I believed in the power of generosity. I never questioned.

I gave.

I was successful in my own spirit. It made me feel good to make others feel good.

I never "gave away the store" despite coming close on days – but I kept the faith.

Mine was a place of refuge.

A place of community.

They were all "my boys."

And my own boys were so good to me.

My boys and daughter had tender hearts as well.

It helped to have a family with giving, tender hearts.

My husband – he was no good. Oh, he was a good man and loved his family, but he loved his drink much more. It got the best of him. It took his young life, and left us, his family, to fend for ourselves.

We did okay – we were people of faith and hope and belief (like you – it runs in our blood), and we were successful in our own right.

My view on success is that success is generosity.

Success is a generous soul.

[Grandmother Mary Ford]

[My paternal grandmother, Mary Ford, delivers a poignant and powerful message as she shares insight on what made her tick. Though she was a member of the hard-timers generation, it appears as if, while counting her blessings, she did what she could to transform those hard times into something a little softer, a tad bit easier. Her essence is gentle, loving, and encouraging.]

Day 31

I don't know much about success, but I do know a lot about separation.

And I do know separation doesn't breed success.

I do know separation leaves you feeling less than lonely.

I don't know much about success, but I do know what it feels like to feel good. Happy.

I guess I just need to talk about feeling happy because that makes me feel good.

I didn't feel good most of the time. I didn't get much reassurance from my mom most of the time. We never really talked about success or all things positive. I mostly listened to all things negative.

I grew up on a steady diet of all things negative. So I guess I can talk about what it feels like to not be successful – which is the opposite of being successful – so by holding a mirror to what I say will reflect success – won't it?

I was mostly happy – make that unhappy.

I was unhappy most of the time, for as long as I can remember.

I think the only time I felt happy was when I could see my life from where I am now, not where I was when I was unhappy.

And for the first time when I was able to see that maybe people loved me, I felt happy, but not so much, because I wasn't able to say anything back to them. (I was unable to respond.)

It's too late when your life is over to say or hear the things we couldn't say or hear before.

Or maybe it's not too late.

I have tried to get messages to my mom – mostly about how I never knew how loved I was – because I was never told in so many words – but I don't know if she ever received my messages, or if she did, if she believed they were from me.

I know she's still not happy, and so I don't believe she would consider herself to be a success. As a matter of fact, I would have to think she considers herself a failure, although she will never let anyone know that.

I imagine I might have been successful as a grown man – on my own, making my own life – living how I wanted to.

But I'll never know. Not in that life time.

It was all too much.

I couldn't think straight.

What I thought were the right decisions – I was told were wrong.

How do you make sense of it all – or sort out the truth? Mostly you know your own truth.

You need to listen to your own voices.

Those voices are the real voices.

The real truth.

I probably would have been successful because I had good voices.

Good thoughts.

Good ideas.

I know that.

My voice was always overpowered – so I gave in, I guess.

Gave up.

Checked out.

It seemed easier.

It wasn't.

[Sean]

[It's been two decades since this young man took his life. He has moved through a great deal of pain and anguish.

From his present vantage point, he is now acutely aware of how loved he is and has always been. Sometimes it is hard to see the forest for the trees. He realizes, in retrospect, there is no way he could have known then what he knows now. That knowing brings him joy.

I have been told he serves as part of a welcoming committee (along with others who have taken their lives) that help other transitioned lost souls feel accepted and loved. This 'work' provides a sense of connectedness and purpose for this young man and the other committee members.]

Day 30

Congratulations! You are officially at the halfway mark. In thirty days my daughter turns sixty-one. Having lived with you through the turbulent days of fighting your demons, I must let you know you are a success!

If you stop and think about what you have been through – the mountains you have scaled despite your uphill battles and the accomplishments you have made – especially around your health – I say you are a success.

You were determined to restore sanity and loving balance back to your life, and I applaud you.

We reflect upon success – it means so much – so many different viewpoints – holds significance in so many different ways – takes on different meanings for each of us.

Success is moving forward.

Whether with small steps or large leaps – it's simply forward motion.

We keep going no matter what.

We don't let anything stop us or get in our way.

Not a cancer diagnosis – or a bout with diabetes or even so far as having a few toes cut off – they're only toes. I still had my feet. I could still walk – and forward I did walk.

You are doing the same, and I am proud of you.

Stick with it.

Whether you can see, feel, or taste it – it doesn't matter. Don't allow anything to get in your way.

I lived forty-three years of my life as a cancer survivor – I lost my breast, but I kept moving – and laughing and enjoying life.

I do know a few things about success, and they don't have anything to do with wealth or money.

Well, personal wealth – that is different. I guess I was a wealthy woman. I still am a wealthy woman.

We are wealthy women.

Keep moving forward.

Don't look back unless it is to remind yourself of where you have been.

Create in the present.

That's all anyone has – the present.

[Leah 'Ma' Ford]

[My mother, Leah, she does know a thing or two about success, and she certainly epitomizes forward movement. My mother maintains an indomitable spirit and continues to nurture and guide me in all things love. I am a blessed woman.]

Day 29

Success is serving others selflessly.

I consider myself a successful soul because I served well. I gave with my heart and my soul and put my family first.

I didn't sacrifice or give up anything – I did what I did out of choice and out of love. My family came first, and my joy was enmeshed in doing just that – caring for my family. It was effortless to take care of my family – even during the most challenging times – the depression, bread lines, coal stoves, and a handful of young ones running around the house.

I loved it.

I loved every minute of it.

Even despite my husband's incessant drinking – I maintained a stiff upper lip – focused on my children, and made the best of it all. I loved my children – even when they argued amongst themselves. Even though our living space kept us on top of one another – I loved my children. And my love and discipline panned out; I raised beautiful children. Soulful.

I guess all families have the proverbial black sheep, and I had a couple of them, but that was okay. They had good hearts and compassion. They may have been lost in their ways at times – but then again, who isn't?

Success. When I reflect back over my life, success would be defined as how you raised your children.

Let me rephrase that – My success is reflected back on the lives of my children – what they became as they grew and the families they raised as they became adults and married.

The love of a person is the most important.

The heart, the soul, the temperament.

It all begins at birth.

The nurturance – nurturing – loving.

You don't need to have much in the way of material things – that which is of value is usually not seen with the eyes.

It is seen with the heart.

You can still be poor and be successful. But then again, what is poor?

Even during our most challenging years I would never have thought us to be poor, although my husband may have told you otherwise.

Wealth and riches come from within.

And I had much of that.

Wealth and riches.

And love.

Plenty of that to give.

My family was my joy.

To this day I remain a successful woman. We have all been reunited, and there is much love to give and receive.

That is success!

[Grandmother Dinah Bibeau]

[Nana Bibeau, my maternal grandmother – she is a warm-hearted, good-natured, love-infused soul. It's no wonder, given her perspective, that my mother, (her daughter) had such a love for children – her own and the many foster children who shared our house throughout the years. Nana was a member of the hard-timers generation. Her resolve to make the best of those times comes through loud and clear. Her generation was often referred to as the "Greatest Generation." I can see why, as love, family, and generosity lit the way in the face of adversity.]

Day 28

Success is going out the way you came in.

[Lucille Ball]

[Her TV sitcom I Love Lucy debuted on the day I was born, October 15, 1951. To this day I resonate with her essence and humor.]

❖ ❖ ❖

It all begins with a stirring in your soul. A spark ignites and you are on your way. It begins at the time of inception – conception.

We agree to the terms of our lives long before we enter into the physical form and we agree to the task which is assigned. It's a long lineage of commitment, and although we are not aware of our commitment, as soon as we take form, it is embedded into our DNA, and so we follow its lead. Our lead. We are one with it. With ourselves. With all. We are one.

We have the free will to decipher for ourselves, to take the path of least resistance, or the path of greatest resistance – we are predestined or programmed to do so – but make no mistake – we have the choice.

The calling is obvious for some and not so for others.

Going to and remaining in the quiet place – the place of reflection, meditation and communion – is essential on a daily, if not more frequent, basis.

It is within that solitude we realign with our DNA – our higher self, our higher purpose.

We are, each one of us, placed here for a particular purpose, and I have found it to be extremely interesting to bear witness to the lives of many veering off course and making choices other than those predestined.

You have an inner compass. We have an inner compass. Most either forget that important element or never connect with that important element. Our compass is centered within our heart. It is wrapped tightly into our emotions and guides us intuitively and instinctively; if only we listen to our compass within. Yes, listen – for it does speak to us. Always.

The truth, our truth, is positioned within our compass within our hearts and will never misguide us. It holds the ideal longitude and latitude of the path of our lives.

Some are set off course so easily and miss the path to success because their minds take control.

The key to "true success" is embedded within the compass within the heart.

That is the secret I reveal unto you today, my great-granddaughter.

Here and now. As I extend my hand, you will notice a tiny gold key. Take it and unlock the door (*so to speak*).

Follow the compass – step aside, seek solitude, and listen – truly listen – yes, to thyself.

We were born with the key to true success.

You have been pointed in the right direction.

Share this with others – it is essential. Especially now.

Allow me to assist you in teaching this.

The Compass Within.

We know the course.

We need to listen.

Make the time and listen.

There is where success has been placed.

[Great Grandmother Vandermölen]

[This is the first connection with my maternal great grand-mother. She appears to be an erudite soul, now doesn't she? Hers is a no-nonsense, to-the-point, universal message. I savor this connection on many levels. Let the teaching begin!]

Day 27

There's an *awful* lot of emphasis being made about success today – almost as if it's a last-ditch effort to find fulfillment before the lights – the proverbial lights are turned off.

It begins with an understanding of one's mind-set, and believe me when I tell you I am far wiser than my years.

We don't give much credence to success in our youth. Well, we, meaning the majority of we.

We skip the light fandango – turning cartwheels on the floor and have a voracious appetite for life.

We eat it up and spit it out.

Fearless – raring to go.

As time marches on we begin to think about settling down – earning a living – becoming successful, which usually translates into having a family, buying a home, earning a decent living, enjoying life.

Then, as the years march on – or move along – when there are fewer years in front of us than behind – there seems to be a need or a calling to listen to our inner desires, and we start to give pause to and actually think about – maybe even entertain – the thought of doing that "something" we once had fleeting thoughts about.

That "something" that we flicked aside and quietly and quickly said no to.

That need or desire – our true self – begins to emerge and becomes extremely attractive. We are no longer able to neither suppress it nor drown it out.

If we're lucky – or adventurous, daring, ballsy, courageous, and have a modicum of belief left – we opt to take that chance.

Go for it.

Pursue that dream.

Make the magic happen.

And our resolve is far greater and more deeply rooted than ever before, because we have less time ahead of us to make it happen.

There's something about a ticking clock that serves as a great motivator.

Something about the sand in an hourglass that gets us moving.

If we are wise enough and poised enough and graceful – we will not panic.

We will simply heed the call and take the steps we innately know we need to take and achieve that success.

'That' success is listening to and following our soul's calling.

If you can hear the slightest of inclinations – please respond – your soul is calling and will lead the way.

[Taborri Spirit Child]

[Taborri Spirit Child, the young soul who is near and dear to my heart. She continues to flit in and out of my readings, bearing truths and spot-on messages. Her playful energy delights and inspires me.]

Day 26

It's no simple feat – mustering up the energy to make a connection.

For some it's effortless – or appears to be effortless – maybe it's the "practice makes perfect" idiom, or maybe it's all about belief.

Believing it is a simple feat – making the connection, that is.

I have been waiting to connect – I have been watching others, but it has been no simple feat.

Success is a "happily ever after."

What does "happily ever after" look like for you?

I thought I knew – thought I had it all planned out – yet life threw me a fast ball. I missed the swing, and it was all over.

Dropped dead in my own backyard.

Up until that point in time, I had been living a "happily ever after."

It's challenging for me to hold this energy. I know I am of the light and in the light, but to reach out and make this connection places me in very bright light. Intense light.

I wonder why?

As I reminisce I am reminded that while I believed I was a success; I had achieved such milestones – wife, mother, forerunner in the women's movement (let's leave it at that) – something was incomplete.

I still don't know what that was? Maybe what I had wasn't enough on some level.

I just couldn't seem to get enough of…what?

I don't know.

I was complete on so many levels – yet incomplete where it mattered most. (My heart?)

I know I'm probably not making much sense at the moment, but, I must tell you – this is a good start for me.

I have seen others do this – reach out and connect – and I have wanted to but wasn't sure I could.

I am. I will fine-tune this.

There are plenty here to help.

I have been a bit of a recluse though – but what I just realized is it is time to reach out.

Maybe I will become complete – find that total success – or love – or joy. I was a joyful woman on the outside.

Imagine how it will be when my outside matches my inside?

It's good to know you can still strive for success – no matter where you are or what form you have taken on, and for that knowing I now feel lighter and more hopeful.

I don't need to go backward – I can move forward. Maybe success is total enlightenment.

Maybe that's what the bright light is all about? Full integration of self with self.

Maybe that's success?

We'll see.

[Anonymous]

[When this feminine energy, whose name we have chosen to withhold for the sake of privacy, came through, she did so with hesitance and feelings of being lost. As we communicated – her speaking, me writing – her energy became clearer and clearer, surer of itself. How beautiful that through this process she has tapped into her voice and shared her feelings, bowing out of the conversation with grace and a sense of surety. Sweet.]

Day 25

Action = Success.

Inaction = Paralysis.

Movement is a necessary ingredient/element in forward motion.

Think about that.

Without movement we remain in place – status quo.

That may work for some.

For others it's a cause for frustration and can be the start of a downward spiral.

We must get outside of our heads and into our bodies and into movement or action.

Too much thinking can cause overwhelm or brain fog and will shut us down faster than you can say "Yankee doodle dandy."

How does one take that first step – the step which will actually bring about that success – which, by the way, is simply a good sense of satisfaction for a 'job well-done'.

Enjoying small bites of success is a great way to fuel you on your way.

Movement creates action, and action puts thoughts into motion.

Having great ideas is great, but they need to be shared to make them real. Otherwise they are ideas only – which serve no one. Well, they will serve to drive you, the thinker, crazy after a while.

Movement is the key.

Begin to move those thoughts around – get them out there to people who can benefit from them.

What is one thing you can do to put those thoughts into action?

Do one thing.

Remember,

Success is best served in small bites
and is simply a sense of satisfaction.

Small satisfactions build, one upon another – and as you build you pick up steam. Before you know it you are a massive freight train chugging up the rail of life, with a well-planned-out map to success in every realm.

You are the driver and conductor.

Let's get this train moving.

Woo! Woo!

[Taborri Spirit Child]

[Taborri Spirit Child has returned to share her straightforward, no-holds-barred wisdom.]

Day 24

I believe the definition of success changes to suit the era and global economy.

While it is the desires of the heart and accomplishments achieved, it is also determined by the signs of the time.

What one person requires and deems successful may not be what another deems successful.

We all require different things.

Healthy children, peace of mind, good neighbors, enough to get by with, harmonious surroundings, and a little time for myself was all I required. And so, because I had days when I was able to have all of that, I felt myself to be a success.

To sit in the kitchen with a cup of tea, watching out over the neighborhood children (mine included) laughing and running about was a great gift to me and one, in retrospect, which made me feel like a queen for the day.

Quiet contentment and security of loving people were the icing on the cake.

We didn't come from much, but we had so much.

The 1950s were an ideal time to be raising a family and settling into a routine.

My neighbors, the other mothers, were around and available for one another. We felt safe and life was full of hope and promise.

It was simpler back then – a slower pace.

Not that we didn't have our own cares or worries – they just didn't feel quite so heavy. They didn't weigh us down.

It was a real community, and we all felt like a million bucks. We were all successful as far as we were concerned – we had it all, and we were sitting on top of the hill.

There wasn't much we required – and we seemed to have the little we did need; therefore, having nothing to desire – we were all successful.

We were all there for one another. Our neighborhood was one big family. I never felt alone.

Now that's a success. So many people are at a loss and are alone these days.

I consider myself a blessed woman to have been born and raised and married and raised my own family during the era in which I did.

I was a smashing success in more ways than one, and I am ever so happy for that.

Memories are fuel for the…I was going to say fire, but there is no fire where I am, and I didn't want anyone to get the wrong idea.

Let me rephrase that – memories are what fuels us – keeps us going.

Count your blessings if you have good memories.

That's surely a sign of success.

[Aunt Yvonne]

[Aunt Yvonne was our good natured, big hearted neighbor of the 1950s. She and her entire family, her husband, John; daughter, Sharon; and son, Donald are all in spirit. Aunt Yvonne's reminiscing brought me right back to my childhood and the many incredible adventures we shared on Arbor Street and Morton Hill Avenue. We were living in a Norman Rockwell painting, or so it felt. The neighborhood was small in size and large on love, present parents, playful sidekicks, and so many opportunities for making mischief. I do count my blessings. Thank you, Aunt Yvonne; I have a bushelful of excellent memories, which include you.]

Day 23

Shine on.

Shine on.

Harvest moon.

Up in the sky.

Do you see what I see?

A Star.

A Star.

Dancing in the night.

With a tail as big as a kite.

With a tail as big as a kite.

Lightness of being – that's success.

NO worries.

Nothing to tie you down, nothing to weigh you down.

Hakuna matata.

Angels can fly because they take themselves lightly.

The key to success is to travel lightly.

It is important to know that no matter where you go you must travel lightly – leave only footprints and harm none.

That's a successful journey.

Balk not.

Keep moving.

Success is knowing when to say enough is enough.

[Spirit Collective]

[A mélange of voices, spirits, and entities flew in on a breeze, sharing a light-hearted message. Collective, conscious, caring, connected – what a welcomed and delightful addition to the mix.]

Day 22

Success is having something to hold onto.

It is a port in a storm, an anchor to keep us from floating off into an abyss.

Success is having someone to depend on. Someone to keep you securely anchored. Someone to let you know everything is really all right, despite what the obvious may be.

We all experience periods of craziness – irrational thoughts and behaviors – but yet – only a successful person will have a point of return. Someone to bring you back when you are so far out there you can't fathom ever coming back.

Despite all of my escapes from reality, sorrow, ill health, horrible thoughts, and bad dreams – I was always able to return to some semblance of normalcy because I had that port in the storm. Aside from – no, in addition to – that port being my mother, who always believed in me even when I know she questioned my sanity, she was always there as my port and my anchor. In addition to her was my faith and belief in Jesus.

I clung to Him through the tumultuous times – he kept me afloat.

Success is a funny thing – elusive – indefinable.

If Jesus was the reason for the season (and he was), success was the substance for the soul.

To believe in yourself and your power, through your faith, that you will make it – no matter what – is a quiet – indescribable, unnamed, nondescript feeling. Bigger than a feeling. More like a fact.

My kidneys went – what did that mean? I'd love to know.

I went within yet without.

I became bigger than myself and my limits – but I also knew how and when to let go.

Let go and let God.

Life on life's terms.

My decision – My death.

It brought me the ultimate in life, in living.

I no longer cling to my faith and to Jesus. I live it. I enjoy it.

I cling to my mother, who you know clings to me. It's all about assimilation. We all know how to assimilate according to our own will. And, yes – we still have free will. It's just so much easier now. No, and I mean *zero*, judgment, which makes exercising our own free will easier yet more challenging because you must rely on your gut instinct or beliefs because there is no judgment. And for those of us who were used to operating from that place we have to learn to operate with a totally new compass, which is very fascinating and a topic of conversation for a later date.

True success is having a port in a storm.

[Anonymous]

[I am personally very proud of this feminine spirit who forced her way through many obstacles to share her feelings and sentiment with us. While she made her presence

quite known to me, we are withholding her name for the sake of her family. I feel her love and light pour through, and that warms my heart. Thank you.

She had questioned what it meant by "my kidneys went." I hope this helps her find solace and understanding: according to Louise L. Hay, "Kidney problems are related to criticism, disappointment, failure, shame. Reacting like a little kid." I trust this explanation will help soothe her soul and provide a sense of direction for possible resolution.]

Day 21

Success is having the courage to speak up for yourself.

It is being able to trust what you have to say is not only worth saying but worth hearing.

I spent much of my life not speaking up for myself – not believing what I had to say had any value.

I barely ever expressed myself. Though I knew I was loved deeply, there was always something missing. Affection? Affection.

I taught my children to suppress their emotions – as I led by example.

It is written "we teach our children by what we say or do not say, not by what we do."

"Do as I say – not as I do."

That expression came back to slap me in the face. Though at the end of my life, all turned out as best as I could expect – you never really prepare...rather, you are never really prepared for end-of-life anything.

You can't make up for all your unspoken truths – feelings – thoughts. Time just doesn't allow for that. So you take them to the grave with you.

What we don't realize – what I never realized – is that the grave is merely an extension of life on earth.

The body goes to the grave.

The spirit remains intact, and you are present with your thoughts and unspoken words. Then, there's just so much to say.

I say this here and now – speak your truths, your thoughts – don't hold back – people need to hear what you are thinking and feeling about them.

Some don't believe in life in the hereafter – What does that mean, anyway – hereafter?

Some don't believe in connecting after you have died. It is then impossible to say what needs to be said.

Your belief is your key to connect. – Block or Blossom – Your choice. You can make the seemingly impossible possible.

We come in dreams; we come in signs – but if you don't believe, we don't have a chance to share what we didn't share when we stood face-to-face, in the flesh.

So be a success now – speak your mind, share your thoughts.

Be courageous.

A postscript: How sweet it is. You hold the key to connection – you may choose to be open to give and receive or remain closed to the possibility. If it is fear that keeps you from connecting, we will help.

[Anonymous]

[My dear aunt, who shall remain anonymous. I love her spunk. Imagine that – offering to help so that others may understand and share the connections. This is amazing!]

Day 20

Comfort, security, love, family – these are some of the elements of a successful life.

Friends, activities, something to always look forward to – to dream about, to make your heart sing – these are some of the elements of a successful life.

Someone to love you and make sure – or, rather, *ensure* – all your needs are and will be met are elements of a successful life.

A loving, caring family, nice surroundings (and not based on monetary niceties, but surroundings which lift your spirits – light, bright, airy).

Faith is of utmost importance, for those who have faith in God are a bigger success than they might realize.

But, then again – it's usually faith which sustains us and keeps us going and makes us feel healthy, wealthy, and wise – even during our darkest hours.

A happy spirit – easygoing attitude – (this, too, shall pass) always lends itself to success – for if you are able to weather any storm, you are truly a success.

And enjoyment.

Always enjoyment.

Find joy in everything you do – yes, even during the challenges and rough spots.

There is always – and I mean always – sunshine on the other side of the clouds. It is easier than you can imagine, walking through the darkness into the light.

Things always get better.

Actually, things are always good. Success, a successful soul – happy-go-lucky and filled with faith – will always look on the bright side of life.

And when experiencing those dark periods, due to ill health, loss of a spouse, friend, or family member, know there is light – always light – on the other side.

A successful soul possesses this wisdom deep within. Even though it may not be first and foremost in their thoughts or mind – it's simply a quiet knowing.

So breathe deeply and relax. We all have what it takes – deep down, within.

I'd like to think we are born with it and then simply forget we have it. It belongs to us.

Look for it. It's there. It's success at its finest – it's the light, it's the love, it's what keeps us going if we simply step aside and allow ourselves to be taken over by that success.

I learned rather late-ish in life that I possessed this quiet, soulful success – although I was always pretty happy-go-lucky.

When I learned of this, it was as if I turned on a light – flipped the switch – began to experience a lightness of being – greater than that which I had experienced before.

So, think about that: **the "success" you seek is within.**

Do you see it?

[Anonymous]

[A beloved "grandmother" and dear friend, whose energy comes through exactly as she did on the earth plane – wise, loving, and extremely grounded. Many of us invest a lifetime seeking that which we already possess – that which dwells within. I am appreciative to you, Grandmother, for reminding us of this gift.]

Day 19

It truly is amazing the number of incarnations we take on in our…

Lifetime?

Many different forms, embodiments, beings:

Human

Canine

Rock

Paper

Scissors

Mineral

Vegetable

Air

Earth

Water

What I'm getting at is you – one – never knows what's next.

You cannot anticipate nor prepare for what's next.

But,

You can prepare for success.

You can prepare for it by being open to receive it.

It all begins with receptivity.

Allowing yourself to be open and (always) in the space to receive.

Now bear in mind – we receive positive and negative. That's a no-brainer.

The success is – or success is – being able to hang onto positive and allow negative to flow right on through.

Think of a colander. When you rinse vegetables or grains using a colander – the water or unwanted particles are the negative. Not needed.

Unnecessary.

Not worth holding onto.

Now don't get me wrong – the water is an important element in the process of rinsing, but you don't need to hold onto it.

Much like receiving negativity, there's a lesson there and a reason why the negativity was attracted or called to you in the first place – check it out – don't dwell there. Bless it, and let it go.

Success is being open to receive.

It is so easy to close down.

It's a form of protection.

I know all about that – especially in my last incarnation as Simone, the ♫ black dog, black dog. ♪

I was abused.

Plain and simple.

I closed down.

That was my lot.

But – I dreamed.

And in my dreams I was loved and respected for who I was and what I had to offer.

I dreamt of that constantly – so much so that I made it happen. I was open to receive – that is what I am telling you.

I was open to receive love and goodness and respect.

And I was blessed with that.

I was blessed – in my third home – by love, respect, and joy.

Much joy.

So success begins with being open to receive.

And a truly successful soul keeps on giving.

Thank you.

[Simone..."Black dog, black dog"♫]

[*Our wonderful, wise spirit dog, Simone. I was moved to tears when her essence came through (again), so loving, clear, and open. Our animal companions and loved ones in spirit speak to us through the language of love. It is incredible to receive Simone's message and it is remarkable to share this space in time with her. I feel her love and know she is with me as she knows we are with her...always. Thank you, Simone!]*

Day 18

'When Pigs Fly' – Now that was a success!

You've gotta love it.

Even from the grave, I soar with success.

Theater, theater everywhere and not a drop we do despair.

Say *what*?

There is success in the theater.

I loved it!

I still do.

I am so excited.

Here's the thing – sometimes we don't realize when we're onto something good.

A natural fit.

I don't know why most of us feel like unless it's uncomfortable or we have to work really hard for it or labor over it until we have worked our fingers to the bone, that it's a good fit. We feel as if anything that comes into our field of vision on a song or a soft breeze or without much thought, work, or struggle must not be so. A good, natural fit, that is.

It must not be the thing we do – or entertain or choose.

Because there was no effort involved.

Imagine that.

Think about how much conditioning we have been through to actually believe in something like that.

I'm here to tell you pigs *do* fly, and they do so effortlessly.

They do so because it comes very naturally for them.

They don't labor over it nor dissect it fifty ways from Friday. They just fly.

They are weightless and formless when they fly and they are as happy as – yes, you guessed it – flying pigs! They're as happy as flying pigs!

We think too much.

We have a tendency, proclivity – you name it – to think too much.

And that weighs us down,

Do you think a flying pig would be a success if he or she actually thought about flying?

Of course not! They'd probably – most likely never get off the ground – and half the fun – if not all the fun – is the feeling of actually flying.

Now that's success!

So move along – get into the fantasy of it all – which is, in actuality – the reality of it all.

We can create wonderfulness from that place.

Do not dwell on the effort necessary to achieve.

The achievement is a by-product of the effortlessness.

Get out there sister and fly with the pigs. (See them smiling.)

Get out there NOW.

[Howard Crabtree]

[Howard Crabtree is yet another two-degrees-of-separation connection and an expressive, creative, enthusiastic energy he is! I saw his co-creation When Pigs Fly, *the musical, back in the mid-1990s. Howard had just transitioned to spirit and his exuberance overflowed throughout the entire production. How fabulous to know his essence has not changed one iota! He's a free-flowing, fun-loving, high flying energy, to say the least!]*

Day 17

Ah, the sweet smell of success.

What do you think that expression suggests?

Do you think it suggests that success has a scent of its own?

Do you think it suggests that success is something that (which) plays on emotions?

The sweet smell of success.

What's the origin?

Is it an expression meant only for those of us with larger-than-life schnozzolas?

Funny, isn't it?

I think there is more to it. Much more to it.

I am of the opinion that success is something which can be experienced through and by all five senses.

Touch, sight, taste, hearing, smell.

In saying that – you will notice that, for me, success was and still is – very sensory.

A sensory perception.

[Pause]

Where am I going with this?

Oh, okay – success being a sensory perception becomes or is very much a part of you – intertwined with each and every fabric of your being.

You must experience it only once – and everybody does at one time or another in their lives – in order to return to that feeling.

We can get back there providing we have experienced it at one time.

We never forget the feeling.

Total peace.

A sense of accomplishment.

And it is a sensory perception because we were all born to be successful.

So when we trigger those senses – it brings us back to that place – those feelings – the ones we were all born with and we *remember*.

It's in the remembering that we are able to re-embody those feelings, which become much more than feelings – they become the fabric of our being once again.

Now please pay attention here:

That fabric – so delicately and beautifully interwoven – never changes – never leaves us; it merely goes to sleep. We forget – but it is there. That's success – our birthright.

When we plug in again – we reignite those familiar feelings. And whammo! All five senses are fired up, and we are living in success.

Don't look for it – See it. (You, Diane, like that expression.)

Step aside.

Smell it – that sweet smell – it's there for the pickings.

[Jimmy Durante]

[What an honor to host Jimmy Durante, one of America's most familiar and popular personalities of the 1920s through the 1970s. He was a singer, pianist, comedian, and actor whose energy came through clear, crisp, and with a sense of humorous authority. Come to find out, The Sweet Smell of Success *is a 1957 American film.]*

Day 16

First and foremost – to thine own self be true.

Easier said than done.

I understand that.

Stick to what you believe.

Trust in what you know.

Through the course of a lifetime, we are pulled in many directions, and if you have a head and a heart full of ideas, it's difficult to choose just one.

I understand that too.

In an effort to – well let me stop here for a minute.

Happiness and peace of mind is what we all want. Bottom line. Deep down or on the surface – we all want to be happy and enjoy peace of mind.

What that looks like boils down to the individual. Because (thank God) we are all different, we each have our own theory of happiness and peace of mind.

It's getting there or being there that's half the fun.

Struggle and challenge comes with the territory. It's our way of learning and lessening our pain.

Staying focused is the key to success.

Because there are so many options, we tend to drift – especially those of us with a creative soul and my blood does run through your veins.

I took on many projects, and I completed many projects because I was focused on the end result. It's easier that way.

As tempting as it was to move on to the next idea, I stayed focused. Well, I'm not the ideal example of a one-project gal – I did begin others while working on the "one," but I completed the "one" before moving on, and that sense of accomplishment made me happy and fueled me to complete the next.

That gave me peace of mind.

Stay focused – you're almost where you want to be.

Stay focused. Completing one project at a time will make you happy, bring peace of mind, and ultimately make you a success.

Advice for today.

[Leah 'Ma' Ford]

[My mother, Leah's fifth "appearance" and I am not surprised...Not only is she my number one, go-to-guide, she sits at the head of my Spirit Support Team board of directors. She is always available, loving and supportive, and shares her sage advice at the drop of a dime. Actually, all I need do is think of her and she appears and offers her guidance or a good kick in the butt, when necessary. Though she is my mother, her advice is timeless and can be heeded by anyone.]

Day 15

Success is raising a family (multigenerational) that you can be proud of.

Living long enough to see your grandchild married is success enough for me – that plus being able to keep a stiff upper lip no matter what.

Being able to rebound and laugh and enjoy life, no matter what, is also a good sign of success.

Keeping your head on straight and standing tall, no matter what – success.

Going on with life after you've suffered the loss of your partner – a mix of faith and perseverance – also translated into success.

Having good, close friends, people you can count on who will be there for you through good times and bad, no matter what – well, you know – success.

Living comfortably, especially during your later years when you can't control your income – success.

That also takes forethought and planning – so you might want to make a note of that.

The last thing you need to be worrying about is money, or other resources – as you age – as the body and mind ages – so make a note of that too.

Celebrating every moment – that is success.

So always find a reason to celebrate everything. Trust me, you don't have to look long or hard – those moments are available and happening every moment – success.

Most of all – have fun. Find the reason or occasion to have fun wherever you can. If you do that, you will definitely be deemed a success.

There is so much worry, despair, grief and unhappiness – if you let it run your life, you will surely go to an early grave, and, trust me – there is plenty of time to go to the grave.

So rejoice – love – celebrate – laugh, and have fun. If you allow yourself those simple luxuries you will surely be a success.

Shalom. Boopa

['Boopa']

[Free spirited, inquisitive, and good-natured, Boopa is the life of any party. Though I did not know her well in form, during our brief and festive encounters, I had the pleasure of sharing her lust for life. Fortunately, she remains with us in spirit, still living the high life! So glad you came through, Boopa. Feel free to return at any time.]

Day 14

Success without struggle.

Accessing your ancestors is definitely success without struggle.

There are so many of you out there. (Yes – to us, *you* are out there – interesting – yes?)

There are so many of you out there who could very easily turn to us for more than just advice. You could turn to us for insight, understanding, and a taste of what life used to be like way back when or just last week.

Too many of you are struggling each and every day, trying to wrap your mind around the current state of affairs, attempting to learn or decipher where you fit into the crazy goings on – you look around and your friends and family members can't make out what is going on, and/nor how they can best leverage their resources. Those dwindling resources.

We are but a breath away. A shot away.

And we are waiting for you to believe, come to your senses, let go of the cynicism or skepticism, and reach out.

We have clear vision and will guide you forward from a past-perception point of view.

We dwell or, rather, access information from our past-perception point of view so that you don't have to.

Create your future, your success, from the present.

Allow us to take care of the past. Allow us to teach you using solid principles from the past.

You will truly be amazed. Or is it you will be *truly* amazed?

We can help you move through and move on to create more happiness and joy in your here and now – so you can make sense of it all.

Understand your role in the big picture.

Find out just exactly where you fit in so you are no longer trying to find your place – so you *will* find your place – and go forth from the place of grounded assuredness.

Being in forward motion truly is a sign of success.

Success without struggle is a letting go, of sorts, a stepping aside and allowing spirit to guide you.

It is very simple.

We speak only the truth because it is all we know from this vantage point.

Imagine being guided and led by such powerful energies?

We are here. We are yours – your family, your lineage, your truth, and hope.

At your disposal.

Believe.

Experience success without struggle.

[Spirit Collective, a collective of caring souls]

[More often than not, I receive messages from a collective force. They are plentiful, wise, and caring. Their voices blend and their messages come together in strong, loving unison. It amazes me every time they come through together, as it epitomizes true harmony and a clear sense of purpose. I am always humbled and grateful for their inspiration, guidance, wisdom, and love.]

Day 13

Grudges do not feed a soul nor do they make a soul successful – do not take grudges to the grave.

We are sometimes fueled by a good grudge. The anger keeps us going. The longer we're angry, the more fuel we have to burn, the larger the flame. The more power we give to the grudge – or holding the grudge – and before we know it, the grudge has completely consumed us, and there's no going back – no putting out the fire.

So my suggestions for a happy, productive life is do not take grudges to the grave.

Forgive, forget, and enjoy life.

Simply signed Edna.

[Edna]

[Though I did not physically meet her, I know her through others who know her well. I had the pleasure of speaking with her from time to time before she transitioned; however, she did not share her pain or her solution until this day. Her advice is timeless and appreciated. She continues to focus on her own forgiveness and the forgiveness of others. Baby steps bring healing results.]

Day 12

Success is making the most of everything you have.

And I mean everything.

Every particle of your being.

Success is not feeling sorry for yourself if you are having a bad day.

Success is tapping into the never-ending well of creativity and love.

If everyone were to choose love to drive their bus – the driving factor in all decisions –the ultimate decision maker – just imagine what a world it would be.

What a wonderful world it would be.

[Referring to the song "(What a) Wonderful World" sung by Herman's Hermits... ♪ "I don't claim to be an A student, but maybe if I were an A student, baby, I could win your love for me." ♪] *

You have to have music in your life.

A song in your heart.

Success is using up every last drop of you before you leave your earthly body.

And I bet you expect me – no, not expect...but I bet you're thinking I might address the earthly body and many of its earthly limitations – but I'm sorry to say I am so free of that; I have moved beyond all of that, and while there may be – or, rather – there are many teaching principles I can use around the restrictions or limitations of the earthly body – I have freed myself and may talk about that some other time – not just now.

I am here to talk about success on a soul level. Taking advantage of every tiny, little particle of your brilliance.

Those tiny particles which hide in the smallest corner of your being.

The tiny particles just aching to be invited out into the light.

Go there – round them up – bring them all together – invite them to come together as a whole.

They want to.

They ache to.

They need an invitation. And they follow direction well, those tiny particles which hide in the smallest corner of your being, just aching to be invited out into the light.

We have a tendency to leave small parts – I like to refer to them as particles – we have a tendency to leave tiny particles scattered here and there within our beautiful being.

In doing so, we remain incomplete.

We are not able to shine our full light.

These particles have split off as a result of trauma, hurt, self-doubt, recrimination, illness, injury, hate, self-loathing, bullying – I could go on forever.

We become fragmented.

As a result – we are less than whole.

As a result – we cannot possibly shine – fully.

That's the key, my friends – to fully shine.

Gather up all those tiny particles – if you don't know how to begin or where to begin, simply sit in silent meditation and scan your body – scan your mind – become your own anti radioactive X-ray machine or MRI or CT scan – whichever you decide.

But – lovingly and patiently – scan.

Call forth and invite those fragmented pieces of yourself to come out – come out and join forces with their brilliant selves.

Boy – you are in for a real treat.

The feeling of wholeness is beyond words.

I could paint about it – paint you a beautiful example – however, I'm not sure how I would deliver that painting to you unless I teach you, Diane, how to translate my paintings. Mmm…something to think about.

Meanwhile, gather up all your tiny particles, and as you do so, feel the intensity of your light shining brighter and brighter as one particle joins another.

You will actually hum.

You will definitely know you are on the right path.

And once you have gathered up all your tiny particles – assimilate and shine!

It is then, and only then, you can use every single ounce of yourself and achieve that success.

Or will you then be the success?

Thanks for the invite. I will return!

All is well.

[Paul Kahn]

[Paul was brilliant energy and an advocate for the physically challenged. He lived his life with grace and pizzazz,

accomplishing more in his lifetime than many accomplish in several lifetimes. Paul lived life on his terms and nothing (and I mean nothing) prevented him from accomplishing all he set out to do. I believe he is on to something, and I say we gather up our tiny particles and shine!]

*♪ Lyrics have been changed to avoid copyright infringements.

Day 11

You can have all the success, fame, and fortune in the world, but if you don't have your health and well-being, you don't have anything.

Health, good health, is the cornerstone to all else.

And believe it or not, it begins in the mind.

In my many years of keeping it as simple as possible or delivering my messages right directly into your living rooms – I sprinkled the mind health in large doses, speaking a language I thought would be the easiest for you to digest.

I made it fun because, after all, no one likes to exercise – oh, let me retract that – few of us love to exercise and stay happy and healthy – I wasn't addressing you – I was addressing those who thought it was too much – a burden – or that you just didn't have the time nor the inclination.

How ingenious to create a program which allowed me to come into your living room and create a real sense of community, all the while intending on creating a healthy movement across the United States.

It caught on like a wildfire, yet many needed constant prodding, inspiration, and motivation.

Many participated just to be a "part of it all."

Many truly, seriously wanted to improve their health and body image, though body image wasn't talked about nor made such a big deal about back then, as it is today.

It seems as if women in particular were too busy raising families and caring for their husbands to really, let me put this delicately – make the time for themselves. Plus there weren't many obese or unhealthy women out there fifty or sixty years ago – even sixty or seventy years ago.

I took on a mission of health and body awareness for personal reasons, and I loved it. I loved every single minute of it.

I made it my personal mission to educate and keep it simple.

People like simple.

People learn from simple.

Through all my fame and fortune, which, by the way, was generated and created from me following my passion – listening to my heart – I relished and cherished my health being my greatest success.

That, my excellent health, kept me going long after the money was redistributed.

My excellent health and the love my wife and I had for each other.

So listen up, kids – please make time to include healthy habits in your success plan.

Remember – it all begins in the mind. Mind over matter, and all.

Plant the seed, then nurture it.

Schedule time for light exercise – or heavy, if you choose that route – and always, always be mindful of how you fuel your body.

Fresh, natural, live, real, clean food.

Always – or the best you can.

It is essential – trust me.

My simple choices kept me alive, vital, and kicking for a very, very long life.

When you are scheduling your meetings and lists of things to do, make sure you are at the top of the list – and

make your life the fittest of all.

That is my simple key to success.

P.S. Discipline and desire required.

You can do it.

Feel the passion and rise, like cream, to the top.

[Jack LaLanne]

[This young man was the forerunner of America's healthy eating and living movement. Jack was an American fitness, exercise, nutritional expert, and motivational speaker

who was sometimes called "the godfather of fitness" and the "first fitness superhero." I am impressed by his simple approach to life, teaching, and learning. I am grateful he chose to participate.]

Day 10

I know it's only fitting that I stop in today – after all, it is the birthday of the wife of my beloved.

I wasn't a success in marriage, but I did know how to love and love well.

The greatest love was the love of self.

You might not understand this, but I loved myself in the moment I took my life.

I knew no other way out from the pain – the never-ending, debilitating pain.

No, I did not think of anyone else as I laid out my plans. And that's my message. Please try to understand.

There's a familiar expression out there, "If mama ain't happy; ain't nobody happy," or something like that – you get the essence – right?

Well, mama wasn't happy. The pain was all-consuming. It left little or no room for any other feelings. There's just no living with that.

Sure, you can say I blame it on the pain (little music here, ♪ blame it on the rain ♫).

All kidding aside – I could very easily blame it on the pain. It was, the pain, that is – that drove me to take my life.

What an odd statement.

I didn't take my life – I ended the pain.

That simple action gave me my life back while it left many, many others in pain.

Their pain passed – as did mine.

Was I successful? That's a loaded question and a topic for conversation at a later date.

I have had a lot of – or a great deal of time [pause]…there really isn't time, per se, here – but there is [pause]…I can't describe it at this moment.

I think back – or, perhaps, just think, as there is no back or forward – there is only now. So let me rephrase by saying I think about my actions and the consequences, and I must say I was successful in ending my pain.

I was successful in loving myself *first* and *enough* to end my pain.

Some may call that selfish. I am here to tell you it was a very loving act and I don't expect anyone to understand – except those who may be experiencing chronic debilitating pain.

Mine was a selfless act – one which I do not promote or advocate.

If I had it to do all over again, would I have done it differently?

Well, here is my response – I honestly do not know.

I feel as if my options were nil – or almost – no, they were – non-existent at the time.

The pain crushed me and my thinking – rational thinking was compromised. At the time, ending the pain was *all* I could think about. It consumed my every waking moment.

If I had been pain-free – NO – I never would have done it; or, yes – I would have done it differently – that goes without saying.

I am here to say I am sorry. I am so sorry. I never meant to hurt anyone. I only meant to remove myself from the hurt.

I can see how "you" may think it was a selfish act – but I am here to tell you it was *selfless* and to **love yourself above all else** is to be truly successful.

I'm sorry to say that.

I feel so much better now.

['Kate']

[It is very important for this feminine energy to share her story, and she pushed through the personal pain to do so. Her transition left many wrought with pain as well, and this,

her apology, is intended to ease everyone's pain (herself included). Reaching out and sharing was a very courageous
step, and I am grateful I was able to help Kate take it.]

Day 9

As for success – I will very simply state – success is a free spirit.

Success is a free spirit.

It is a feeling deep within that anything is possible and everything is possible.

It begins with a deep belief in yourself.

Realizing many are challenged these days – with how to deeply believe in themselves – I offer this advice:

There was a time and place in everyone's life when you did something – perhaps an act of kindness – or provided loving advice for a friend or performed a selfless act or deed for a stranger – without even giving thought to what you (they) were doing. Your thought – those words, deed, act, profoundly shifted the other person's life.

In that act and that shift you (they) were in their full place of belief in themselves (an unconscious state of being).

Do you remember the last time an event or act similar to what I am saying took place?

If so, connect with those feelings.

The feelings you felt – the feelings the other person felt.

Good.

Reassuring.

Comforting.

Solidifying.

Grounding.

Loving.

You (they) were operating from that place of deep belief.

We are all capable of connecting with *that* place within.

We sometimes lose sight of that place (it's so easy to ignore) in the hustle and bustle of life. And if left in darkness for too long, a fungus will grow – similar to the life of a mushroom.

So reconnect with that place and soar from that place.

If you aren't quite sure how to soar – yet – reconnect with that place and take small steps to love that part of yourself.

It is from that place – love, confidence, and freedom grow.

Those are essential ingredients to fostering a free spirit.

A free spirit is unencumbered.

Confident in its own beauty and light – all it wants to do – a free spirit's mission – is to fly free and share its beauty and light.

And there is no better feeling in the world.

That's pure success at its finest.

Flying free with beauty, light, love, while helping others to do the same in the process.

That's our purpose.

Our divine purpose.

We can teach that or live that from any plane of existence – or, rather, from *every* plane of existence.

You may be wondering how I transitioned – considering my abrupt departure.

I was shocked.

Then comforted and loved. Totally loved.

So loved that all else faded away. So loved that all else was crowded out.

You too are so loved.

It's probably unimaginable how loved you are, especially by those who have left their earthly bodies.

Oh, we love, and we love strong and deep.

We are present and available, and, yes – we do watch over you.

While we cannot control outcomes, we can work our magic, and we love to love.

So live, love, fly free – and allow your free spirit to soar.

['KD']

[Another "six degrees of separation" connection who came through replete with softness and love. Her death was tragic and brutal, yet her spirit remains loving and encouraging. There is so much to be said for those in spirit. Their community is full of grace, truth, unconditional love, and desire to reach out and connect. Thank you, KD. Thank you for sharing and for letting us know all is well.]

Day 8

Success is not a destination (or a place); it is a state of being.

There are no winning formulas – no methods to follow, no methodology to achieving success.

Many have attempted to create blue prints – simple steps – action plans – all to no avail.

There are no steps to success.

Success is not a destination. What it is – SUCCESS – that is – is a state of being.

Success is a state of being.

Think about the many times in your life you have ventured out on a journey with a special destination in mind.

For example – crossing the Nairobi Desert to reach Jerusalem. You know your start point, and you know your end point. If you planned well and factored in all the variables, you knew what it would involve to reach your destination.

You would have to calculate the number of miles you would travel and convert those miles into the number of hours or days it would take to travel the distance, which would be determined by your mode of transportation.

Then you would have to determine, based upon the amount of time it would take – what type of supplies and how much you would need.

Food, clothing, shelter – the basics.

If animals were your mode of transportation – you would have to calculate and prepare for their needs as well.

There would be a great deal of conversation and preparation involved in the process – before you even took your first step.

Achieving success is quite the contrary.

There is no planning – not in the formulation state.

It's more of an unfolding of your nature.

Very different.

The unfolding of one's true nature is all about nurture, love, and belief.

Belief in your genius – yourself.

Many looked upon me as a genius – I was simply operating from my place of passion.

I wasn't a genius in the true sense of genius.

I was (and remain to this day) a happy-go-lucky fella who loved living in the questions.

That kept me alive and thinking. I questioned and in the questions birthed new ideas which brought forth new questions.

Do you see where I'm going with this?

I hadn't planned nor prepared for "reaching success."

It was created as a by-product of me taking advantage of my full faculties. And I truly enjoyed taking advantage of my full faculties – believe me.

I drank up every ounce of it – and the cup never ran dry. It's amazing; the more you drink the more there is available to drink.

It's actually quite amazing, and, yes – my cup runneth over.

Approach the thought of success without much thought, and you will find you are smack-dab in the middle of a successful string of consciousness, and you will be living the highlife.

[Albert Einstein]

[This male energy came through with a straightforward confidence. He had something to share, and share he did. I was quite blown away when he reminded me of $E=mc^2$ and signed off as Albert Einstein. His energy is heady and ethereal, grounded and practical.]

Day 7

Success can usually be seen through the eyes of your friends and family – actually – through the eyes of your family first – your spouse. That's all that really mattered to me.

I could always gauge the level of my success by the way my wife looked at me when I returned home from a hard day's work.

Most of the time supper was ready. That meant she was proud of me and wanted to show that pride to me as best she could. A well prepared meal with my family by my side. That's what made me feel successful. I felt like I had it all. And "back then," in the fifties mostly – "all" was a roof over our heads, food on the table, a job we could get up each morning and go to – a family to return home to. That was always a good day.

We didn't want much – just a little more than what we were accustomed to – yet we knew we had it all if we had a home, food, job, and family and not necessarily in that order.

Family also extended beyond immediate. Beyond wife and children. Beyond to siblings, parents, friends.

It was so simple – hard work, but simple – or so it felt.

Slow and steady was the key. We weren't in a hurry, didn't need "things" *right there and then*. We accepted the things we had, and strived for something a little bit better.

Success wasn't a term lightly used or even discussed – really.

We knew we had a good life – *"the life of Riley"* – and because we had the basics, we had it all.

So if you want to know if you are successful, **look into the eyes of your spouse** – husband – wife – that special someone – and see what they see.

[Uncle Eddie]

[My uncle Ed shared a simple philosophy, which was shared by many who raised a family during the 1950s and 1960s.

Having modern conveniences, such as refrigerators and televisions, really made us feel like kings and queens. 'The Life of Riley' was a TV Series, which ran from 1953 to 1958. The expression, "living the life of Riley" suggests an ideal, contented life.]

Day 6

Success is knowing when to throw in the towel.

[Uncle W., wishing to remain partially anonymous]

[He was a man of few words in life and remains a man of few words in the afterlife.]

❖   ❖   ❖

Ah, the sweet smell of success.

Success is knowing when to throw in the towel.

It's knowing when enough is enough and when it's time to step aside.

I had always considered myself a successful man. Despite my spells (seizures) – which really took a toll on me.

I lived in a nice house and had a wonderful, attentive, loving wife. Everything I could possibly imagine. Great family, great friends, enough money to do what we wanted and live out our dreams – vacations – swimming pool right outside our door, plenty of spirits – the kind you drink, that is – and not so much as a care in the world. Except, as I mentioned, my seizures.

But we lived a good life, good jobs, money, and we were both successes in our own right.

However, the universe, God, call it what you'd like – had different plans. Heck, we even visited the Vatican and got to kiss the pope's ring (for two thousand bucks). My wife went to mass every single day. Success at its finest.

This is interesting – as I began to speak and share, I felt a bit like a cynic. Now that I hear myself and take a good look around me, I actually feel like I am "seeing" things clearly for the first time since my arrival.

I can see we were chosen and are a success *still* because we are sitting at the right hand of God. Amazing how I just received that clarity and am now feeling lighter and brighter.

Success is knowing when to step aside in more ways than one.

When I stop to think about it – we still do have it all.

Just not within the confines and constraints we had been so accustomed to...

Form.

Matter.

It takes some getting used to – energy, pure energy.

Yet I can feel it now – the success all around me. Warmth, love, joy, community.

There is a sense of loving community.

My wife is busy – administering her profound love and advice to others – a nurse, of sorts.

She was my perfect nurse. Still is, I can see. Not for me though. I no longer need her in that capacity.

So thank you for helping me to see that I am still a very successful man.

I lost nothing.

I gained so much more.

[Paul W., wishing to remain partially anonymous.]

[What an honor to have helped create and hold the space in which Paul was able to reflect on his own life/afterlife and see his situation from different perspectives. I am comforted to know he accepts the love that surrounds him and feels supported enough within his community to trust himself to share. Thank you, Paul!

P.S. Remarkable! Spirit never ceases to amaze me. Paul picked up and expounded upon Uncle W's sentiment "success is knowing when to throw in the towel".]

Day 5

Conviction.

Fortitude.

Desire.

[Taborri Spirit Child]

[Dropping in once again.]

❖   ❖   ❖

Stop second-guessing yourself.

Take it from me.

Here are the brassy facts from a gal who always second-guessed herself – that is, up until the time I knew I didn't have the time to second-guess myself.

Oh sure, I would have used the rest of my "allocated" or "allotted" time second-guessing and God knows I used precious minutes with the "shoulda, coulda, wouldas" but it wasn't until the sense of urgency slapped me in the kisser that I knew whatever I had wanted to achieve or get done and had been doing a good job of holding back and second-guessing myself about, I needed to just jump in with both feet and say what the hell!

Don't beat yourself up.

We earthlings invest so much time second-guessing that we actually steal precious minutes from ourselves.

Imagine that image – a cat burglar all dressed up in black – mask, hat, and all – sneaking through an alley and peeking through a window – looking at herself and wondering how she can get in there and steal more of her precious time.

While we don't do that on a conscious level – we do *do* that! So cut it out.

Stop second-guessing and stealing precious moments. Just do it. They'll be plenty of opportunities to refine or decide if you want to do something else entirely different.

You know you are on the verge of something big when you hesitate.

At least that was true for me.

That's one of the reasons I decided to come through and add some more of my star-like two cents from here:

One: Because I can.

Two: Because I love you.

Three: Because I don't waste precious time anymore, which is funny because we have so much of it – but it's not called time.

More like eternity. Imagine that.

You may have eternity when you join me in this form. But for now – use every single, solitary minute doing what you love.

Don't labor – deliver.

Deliver that baby now.

Tee hee.

[Candace Hopkins]

[My good friend and confidante, Candace, sprang into action and returned to add her two cents by announcing, "I'd
like to come back, if I may, it looks like you need help." Our
friends and loved ones in spirit are so present and willing to
lend a hand at the drop of a dime. How wonderful for us;
how rewarding for them. The best advice I can offer (and I
find myself doing so over and over again) is don't look for
them – see them! They want to be of service.]

Day 4

The beauty of success is that *you*, and only *you*, get to define its meaning.

No one else can tell you what success means nor tell you what the appropriate level of success is for you.

We all have our journeys in life, and we get to define the momentous moments along the way – don't let anyone ever tell you that you don't have the right to define your own moments.

Success can be something as simple as watching a breathtaking sunset on an otherwise crappy day. And it can also be signing a multimillion dollar record deal.

That's the thing – you get to decide and tag what you deem successful.

Success is also determined by the role you play in life – what you do for a living – how you make your money.

A housewife raising three kids and caring for her husband might consider herself a success at the end of each day.

A performer who closes his act for the day – a flawless act – might consider himself a success.

Again – you get to decide.

Success to others is showing up.

Just the simple act of showing up – putting your best foot forward.

There are so many variables when considering or talking about success.

Everyone I ran with in my day – my circle of influence – all considered themselves a huge success. It wasn't too hard to do that – in those days – in the heydays.

So be careful when talking about or trying to define success.

It can be so many different things to so many different people. It takes on a different meaning for each individual.

Bottom line is – whatever you believe constitutes success *is* success, and no one can take that away from you.

['Ol' Blue Eyes']

[This melodic male spirit entered onto the scene with very "rough" energy. As he continued to share, his energy became far mellower, especially by the end of his visit. He referred to himself simply as Ol' Blue Eyes, and I appreciate his to-the-point message of success. No muss. No fuss.]

Day 3

Success comes in many shapes and sizes.

It disguises itself and leads you to believe it is everything you could possibly want.

It's elusive, insidious, and enticing.

Success pretends to be your friend – as it goes from person to person collecting souls.

Why am I telling you this?

Forewarned is foretold, and foretold is power, just as knowledge is power.

Oh, and by the way, success is quite an aphrodisiac. It can entice you to do things you would never have dreamed possible.

It's a rush.

It's a high.

It is always manageable if you have the knowledge, and that is why I am here.

I am here to share my knowledge, experience, and wisdom.

Do not allow success to suck you in – take success at face value and allow it to come to you on your terms.

In small, slow doses it's manageable and can do wonders for inspiring you to move forward.

Learn how to manage *it*.

Do not let it manage *you*.

I have witnessed many, many people who were swept away by or on the wave of success, and they never returned.

What I mean by that is that they never returned to the person/people they were.

They were seduced by success and became success's slave. They lost themselves to success, all the while leading others to believe they had it all and that they were happy.

Trust me – unmanaged success breeds unhappiness.

It *is* manageable, and you can have it all – you need to find the balance.

Stop when you begin to feel intoxicated – or, better yet – don't allow yourself to reach the point of near intoxication. That is a slippery slope.

Determine what success will look like for you and what you are willing to do to achieve it.

Then map it out.

This is the important step.

You have got to map it out.

Be in charge.

Know how much you want – first know how much is how much – too much, or otherwise – then go for that. Make *that* your goal.

And monitor it so you are taking it in exactly at the pace and amount *you* want and have planned for.

When success comes to you like a tsunami – it can kill you. I don't mean literally – I mean figuratively.

I have lost too many of my dear, close friends to this disease – success.

Oh, don't get me wrong – success is wonderful.

You just need to know how much is enough and what your plan is for achieving that much over a certain period of time and then just execute your plan believing you will achieve.

Manage it.

Don't let it manage you.

[Mama Cass]

[Words of wisdom from a woman who sang of words of love. ♫ "You oughta know by now." ♫ I am deeply touched

and honored to have channeled this powerful, meaningful mama energy. Boy, they know no limits when it comes
to delivering and sharing messages. Wowza, Mama Cass,
thank you. There are no "worn out phrases" ♪ here!]

Day 2

Success is a series of accomplishments.

It is something upon which you build.

A strong foundation that/which is structured brick by brick.

You may have learned by now that success means many things to many people.

It has a life of its own and takes on a meaning of its own.

It is perceived in the eye of the beholder.

I am of the opinion that success is continually building upon itself.

It is a tool one can use to ground themselves and motivate themselves.

It can be served up in small doses and therefore be easily digestible or come on fast and furious and totally overwhelm.

We each take away what we need in the pursuit of achieving success. I do, however, feel success is emotionally based – not so much a thing we place on the mantle but a feeling we feel for a job well done. A quiet contemplation or reflection for a long-held dream we have finally put into action and achieved.

The feeling of "that a girl!"– which we experience when we know we have _____ (fill in the blank).

Arrived at.

Achieved.

Accomplished.

What you choose.

It's your choice.

You choose, and that's the beauty of it.

You get to choose.

We all possess the power and potential to achieve our own sense of true accomplishment.

That, my dear, is what I refer to as **the true essence of success.**

That feeling or knowing that we could have achieved whatever it was we had been thinking about, dreaming about, longing for...long before we put that thought, feeling, emotion into action and then, after taking that action and reaching that goal.

The *feeling* of what we have accomplished.

The *knowing* of what we have achieved.

That's my definition of success.

[Jean Gorman]

[My greatest mentor, Jean Gorman, has always lifted my spirits. She has influenced my life at such a deep, rich level. I was a hard-working, curious, young women possessing a

great deal of spunk and rising through the ranks of corporate America when I was taken under her wing. I questioned everything – especially authority. She was unphased and determined to teach me the ways of the corporate world. Her office walls, painted the color pink, were covered (and I mean top to bottom with little or no space in between) with plaques replete with positive affirmations long, long before positive affirmations were chic or all the rage. (The color pink, according to Jean, inspired positive thinking.)

She led by example, didn't hesitate to pass out warm fuzzies or tough love. How fitting she has chosen to come through once again at the finish line of my project. I know she celebrates this accomplishment with me. Thank you, Jean. I am grateful you remain dedicated to my success.]

Day 1

Success is a job well done!

Congratulations on a job well done!

I reserved the right to have the last word, so to speak, as it is the eve of your sixty-first birthday and a milestone in your life.

A lesson well taught and well learned. Completion.

Completion is a great part of what fueled my life. Setting goals and completing them.

You know how list writing was important to me – it helped to keep me focused and it helped me to keep my eye on the prize (the sense of completion), but more *importantly* – it set up a system in which I could congratulate myself each and every time I crossed something off the list.

There is nothing more motivating than having a sense of accomplishment, and crossing a task off a to-do list is the perfect way to do that.

You have been questioning for years – who motivates the motivator. You began to do so when you were first promoted to a managerial position in your mid-twenties – a big accomplishment, by the way!

While you questioned that with humor and as a means of getting your point across – you often wondered – who motivates the motivator?

Well, here's a gift for you, my dear daughter – the answer…

The motivator motivates the motivator.

And the crossing off of a task on your to-do list is the perfect way to make that happen.

The big point I'm making is you can now cross off your list "writing your first book" and go on to building momentum.

This advice isn't directed solely to you. It is universal advice and can be applied to everyone.

The first step is always the hardest to take.

We can give ourselves a thousand reasons why we can't take it – yet what it usually boils down to is we're afraid.

There's no need to be afraid of anything – not even death. It's not all it's cracked up to be.

It's in the living and being that true success is found.

Each moment is priceless – do not squander one moment.

Reflect back on the words of wisdom contributed by many brilliant, heartfelt, and special souls who came through to help you achieve this goal.

What goes around comes around – you live by that – continue to do so.

You make me proud – and I stand ready to continue to help you along your journey.

To many and all, I say – keep your eye on the prize.

Never lose sight of what makes you happy.

And please know – not only is it okay to seek happiness and pursue it – it is important. It is imperative you do so.

It is in the pursuit of that happiness that you find happiness, and it is in the living of happiness that success dwells.

So go forth – continue your pursuits and know that I – know that *we* – are here to guide and support you every step of the way. Happy Birthday, Diane. I love you! Ma.

[Leah 'Ma' Ford]

[What an appropriate ending to such a collective, heart-warming endeavor – my mother, my guide. She is with me all the way, closer now than ever. Thank you, Ma. Thank you, one and all.]

THE JOURNEY'S END...or is it just the beginning?

Thank you for investing your time and energy communing with those in spirit. They are grateful to you for "listening." Were their perspectives on success what you had expected? After reading their stories, would you answer the first four questions any differently?

Do you consider yourself a success in your own eyes? If so, describe what that looks like and what feelings are associated with being successful. If not, what will it take for you to achieve success (e.g., meaningful relationships, deeper love of self, more money, etc.)?

_____

_____

_____

_____

_____

_____

_____

_____

_____

_____

How easily do you allow another's definition or perception of success to define you, influence your actions, and impact your lifestyle? How does that feel (e.g., authentic, overwhelming, expansive, joyful, contracting, or satisfying)?

_____

_____

_____

_____

_____

_____

_____

_____

_____

_____

_____

_____

_____

_____

_____

_____

_____

_____

_____

_____

What are the little things in life you may have a tendency to overlook in your efforts to strive for success?

_____

_____

_____

_____

_____

_____

_____

_____

_____

_____

_____

_____

_____

_____

_____

_____

_____

_____

_____

_____

_____

_____

_____

_____

If you have yet to achieve the level of success you know is possible, what will it take to do so, and how will you know when you have achieved that desired level? In what ways will your life change, what will you feel and look like, and how will those around you be impacted?

_____

_____

_____

_____

_____

_____

_____

_____

_____

_____

_____

_____

_____

_____

_____

_____

_____

_____

_____

Please jot down any new insights, ideas, action plans, or thoughts that will help you to gain a clearer perspective on your quest to achieve personal or professional success.

_____

_____

_____

_____

_____

_____

_____

_____

_____

_____

_____

_____

_____

_____

_____

_____

_____

_____

_____

_____

_____

_____

_____

_____

Now please jot down your thoughts on those areas of your personal or professional life where you feel guidance from your ancestors, loved ones, and/or me will help jump-start you into action, gain clarity, and move you closer to your success.

_____

_____

_____

_____

_____

_____

_____

_____

_____

_____

_____

_____

_____

_____

_____

_____

_____

Diane Marie Ford, Certified Holistic Counselor,
Spirit Medium

Info@TheSpiritsSpeakSeries.com

Diane Marie Ford specializes in connecting people here on earth with those in the afterlife. As a holistic counselor and spirit medium, she blended her spirit-strong abilities with her corporate-savvy, interpersonal skills to connect, communicate and write *The Spirits Speak on Success*. She is co-founder of and contributor to *In Your Own Words Women*, a collaborative book series. Ford is founder and CEO of Listen to Thyself: holistic counseling and revolutionary conversation with spirit (ListentoThyself.com); a columnist, poetess, blogger, avid writer and a contributing author in *365 Life Shifts*.

She lives with her wife, two dogs, several rescued cats, a flock of hens and one handsome rooster in southeastern Massachusetts. *The Spirits Speak on Success* marks the debut of Ford's series, *The Spirits Speak*.

In Diane's words; *"I communicate with those in spirit through various senses. I see images. Sometimes the images are as clear a photograph and include many details about the person or place. Other times the image is blurry yet replete with information. I sense energies. I feel and take on emotions of those who connect. I become filled with joy, sadness, apprehension, or whatever emotion those in spirit impart at the time. I hear them speak and have been told theirs is the language of love, not words. (They sound like words to me.) Once in a blue moon I will smell a scent;*

the smoke from a cigar, or cigarette, perfume, or a baked good. I do not profess to know how communication is possible, but I do know it is possible.

My mission in life (and who knows – perhaps in the afterlife) is to be of service to both those in spirit and those on the earth plane (who want to connect with those in spirit). I am a compassionate advocate of healing the 'ties that bind us' by connecting with the energy and essence of our ancestors and loved ones in spirit while helping them connect with us to foster communication and conversation. My focus is on deepening relationships, reducing pain and suffering and sharing the love."

Author's Note

The information provided by the spirits was recorded verbatim and taken at face value. All the information in this book is published in good faith and for general information purposes only. I do not make any warrantees about the completeness, reliability, and accuracy of this information. Any action you take upon the information in this book is strictly at your own risk. I am not liable for any losses or damages in connection with your use of the content herein. Information contained herein is protected under Fair Use in the Copyright Act.

I do not dispense medical advice or prescribe the use of any technique as a form of treatment for physical, emotional, or medical problems without the advice of a physician, either directly or indirectly. My intent is only to offer information of a general nature to help you in your quest for emotional and spiritual well-being. In the event you use any of the information in this book for yourself, which is your constitutional right, I, the author and the publisher assume no responsibility for your action.

Thank you for reading this book. 'We' hope our messages nourished you and helped you to better understand the power and purpose of connection, communication and love, while assisting you in living a deeper, richer, and more successful life now, in the present.

Made in the USA
Columbia, SC
01 August 2017